Praise for *The Light Giver*...

"What fun it is to follow Reb Bahir's rabbi-hero on his journey through the Wild West and the Jewish calendar. A wonderful read, it sneaks in solid teaching wrapped in a rollicking tale."
— Rabbi Zalman Schachter-Shalomi, author of *A Heart Afire*

"Jewish mystical stories were born at the strange, hazy crossroads between uncommon wisdom and common sense. *The Light Giver* hearkens back to the time when rabbis didn't lecture from podiums and write blog posts from iPads, but went on adventures into the wild, befriending runaway slaves and dodging Injun arrows, throwing themselves into the wide world because G-d created it all. Written in the fine tradition of Reb Shmuel Munkes and *The Frisco Kid*, the stories in this book are funny, sad, innocent and world-weary, and truly, truly wise."
— Matthue Roth, author of *Yom Kippur A Go-Go: A Memoir*

"At once funny, touching, and profound, *The Light Giver* takes us on a journey through the Jewish calendar, the Jewish spirit and into the Jewish soul. Rabbi Davis is by no means conventional, and this book is unlike any other. Within it there are sparks of Divinity waiting for us to unearth. This book is a delight to read and learn from."
— Mayim Bialik, actress and author of *Beyond the Sling*

II

The Light Giver

The Holy Adventures of
A Hasidic Jew in the Old West

Explorations of the Holy Days of the Jewish Year

Bahir Davis

Albion
Andalus
Boulder, Colorado
2012

*"The old shall be renewed,
and the new shall be made holy."*

— Rabbi Avraham Yitzhak Kook

Copyright © 2012 by Bahir Davis
First edition. All rights reserved.

No part of this book may be reproduced or transmitted in any form or by any means, electronic or mechanical, including photocopy, recording, or any information storage or retrieval system, except for brief passages in connection with a critical review, without permission in writing from the publisher:

Albion-Andalus Inc.
P. O. Box 19852
Boulder, CO 80308
www.albionandalus.com

Design and composition by Albion-Andalus Inc.
Cover design by Albion-Andalus Inc.
Cover illustration by Netanel Miles-Yépez.

Manufactured in the United States of America

ISBN-13: 978-0615611198
ISBN-10: 0615611192

"It is a story that I heard from the Black Hat, the White Man who would visit with my father. He would come, and some of the people would share stories of our people and he would share stories of his. He loved hearing our stories and he learned them. He treated us with respect, and so we treated him in the same way."

— Strong Wind, "To Remember the Stories"

Contents

Acknowledgments
A Note to the Reader

The Holy Journey	1
The Unexpected Guest (*Shabbat*)	13
The Shelter of Peace (*Sukkot*)	27
The Miracle of Rededication (*Hannukhah*)	41
Encircling the Enemy (*Hosha'anah Rabbah*)	69
Crossed Dreams, Shared Visions (*Yom Kippur*)	77
Freedom in the Wilderness (*Pesah*)	87
The Days of Awe (*Rosh HaShanah*)	103
The Tree of Life (*Tu B'Shvat*)	117
A House of Prayer for All People (*Shavuot*)	137
To Remember the Stories (*Purim*)	155
A Guide to the Jewish Holidays	163
A Jewish Calendar	175
About the Author	176

Acknowledgements

I WISH TO THANK THE KIDS of all ages who have helped me find in my soul the words to write this book. To all the students over the years who enjoyed my stories and interpretations; to my friends in Crested Butte who have let Hedvah and me into their homes and hearts; to the members of SEFTY who were my teachers, who always encouraged me to share, and gifted me with their compassion and confidence, I am very grateful.

To friends, who offered me shoulders on which to cry, ears to hear my ramblings, mouths whispering advice when I needed it most and *tzedaka* to allow me to finish this work: My brother, Rabbi Michael Davis; Reb Hersh McCall, and Devorah McCall, of blessed memory; Steve Mertz; and Rebbetzin Eve Ilsen, storyteller and musical Muse whose laughter rings joyously in my ears; and to so many others, my deepest thanks. To Topher and Alice who read and critiqued with compassion, I appreciate your kindness and caring. And I would like to thank the tribal folk, and friends of the tribes, who have welcomed and taught me over the years; most especially, Harold Whitehorse, Bill, Ash and Ayelet Perry, who brought and allowed me to Sundance and be "pierced to the Tree of Life."

To the older and younger 'kids' who have touched my heart and soul, and who are my spirit guides:

Rabbi Abraham Cronbach, my grandfather, who, when I was young, told me Bible stories in words and in a way that helped me understand their depth and power;

Rose Cronbach, my grandmother, at whose kitchen table I filled my body and my soul, from whom I learned of gentle compassion for all people;

Rabbi Maurice Davis, my father, who sat with me in the evening and recited with me the *Shema* which guided me, led me to gentle sleep, and who always had advice and a hug;

Marion Davis, my mother, who has always been there to listen and laugh and cry with me;

Ronin Davis, my son, whose depth and beauty inspired me to find the gentle wisdom within the Jewish tales that I shared with him when he was young, and which guides him today with his commitment and sensitivity to others;

Talia Davis, my daughter, who has inspired me from day one with the openness of her spirit quest, her depth of soul, with her humor and strength, and her quiet, powerful, "I love you Tattisan";

Barak (Gage) Schaub, who challenged me, encouraged me, argued with me and laughed with me;

Iana Davis, my chosen sister, my 'nudgetive' who has encouraged me to continue my writing, and who proofread the manuscript;

Malka Tzedek and Mark Culver, who bring to life the words *Garei Tzedek*, for whom righteousness is simply a way of life;

Netanel Miles-Yépez, my editor, publisher and friend, for his editing skills, his great wisdom in seeing that these stories would make a good book, and for his moral support when I felt that they would not;

Rabbi Zalman Schachter-Shalomi, my Rebbe, mentor and dearest friend, who gives me his laughter and tears and his support in everything that I do and without whom this book would never have been written;

Hedvah Rahamyah Davis, my belovedest, who has encouraged me with love and light, who has stuck with me through thin and thinner and whose laughter brings life.

— BAHIR DAVIS, Lafayette, Colorado

A Note to the Reader

HISTORY DOES NOT EXIST. What exists are accounts of history. What really happened is rarely written down in the sense of pure fact. Every writer interprets; every speaker colors the facts. Some interpret and color through the vagaries of personal memory. For instance, my brother and I remember our lives together quite differently. Our minds have subtly changed our memories of events. And most, if not all, historians have their own point of view which comes out in their writing. Having said all that, I love history. I have a fondness for the history of the United States and especially the West (myths and 'mythtakes' included). I grew up with stories of America, of the hunters and gatherers, the mountain men and first tribes, of gunfighters, lawmen, of 'Cowboys and Indians,' and they hold a special place in my heart. It was a great joy to bring some of the history, culture and faith of my tribe into the same venue as these, the tales with which I grew up.

Throughout this work, I have referred to Native Americans or First Nations peoples as 'Indians,' and in some cases, 'Injuns.' For when Columbus arrived in this part of the world, he was a little confused; he thought that he had reached India, and therefore, referred to the indigenous people as 'Indians.' The name took, and until the age of 'political correctness,' the tribal peoples of this land were called Indians. Most Native Americans whom I have met would prefer not to be called by any generic name, but rather by their tribal names, whether it is the Americanization of their name or the original name. For example, there is a powerful and spiritual people who live in the Southwest who call themselves the N'de, but are generally known by the Zuni or Hopi word for 'enemy,' Apache. Further North and East is a tribe who refer to themselves as Lakota, but who are often called by the French name, Sioux. Be that as it may, Euro-Americans (keeping with the PC platform), first referred to all members of all tribes by the misnomer created by Christopher Columbus—Indian. The less educated soon slurred the word into the slang 'Injun.' From my research, I gather that it was not meant to be offensive, but merely descriptive. In this book, I have used it to create a sense of authenticity.

But even as I tried to maintain authenticity with regard to American modes of speech and the pronunciation of the time, I did not do so with my character's Hebrew. The transliterated Hebrew in this book follows Sephardic pronunciation, while Reb Ya'ir would certainly have used an Ashkenzai, or Eastern European pronunciation. I chose the Sephardic pronunciation for teaching purposes, as this is the pronunciation taught in modern Israel, in academic programs, and in many Jewish day-schools. One of the hidden agendas of this work is to encourage an awareness of the Hebrew blessings of the Jewish tradition, to help people to learn them through the stories and eventually to take them into their hearts.

The Holy Journey

THE COLD SWEPT across the floor of the *yeshiva* and climbed up the bodies of the young men studying Torah.* They looked up to see a boy rushing through the door with something in his hand, yelling "A letter from America!" He handed it excitedly to the young rabbi sitting with his students. The students seemed to share the boy's excitement and looked expectantly at the rabbi who simply put it aside and continued his teaching. But the students weren't willing to let it go that easily. "Nu?! Nu?!" they nudged him.

He smiled at their curiosity and gave in. "Okay, I'll open the letter . . . *if* you'll promise that we can get back to our studies after I share it with you."

He fully expected that the note from the congregation in that far away and strange sounding land called 'San Francisco' would contain a rejection. After all, they must have had hundreds of rabbis from all over Europe vying for that position; it promised adventure, and the inner adventure of finding one's personal path. Who wouldn't want to experience the wonder of travel and serving a congregation in the New World? All of the P'shyskha

---

* A *yeshiva* (place of sitting) is a study hall or school in which students study Torah (guide/teaching), referring to the first five books of the Bible. However, in a more general way, Torah refers to the entire body of sacred Jewish writing, and even the path of the Jewish people itself.

2

Rebbes had taught that it was the goal of all *Yidden* to fly from falsehood and to experience the quest for authenticity that is the inheritance of every individual.* Many rabbis greater than Reb Ya'ir must have applied for this wonderful chance to be involved in that very quest for authenticity. So, with so many great rabbis competing, why would this congregation hire a young, inexperienced, wet-behind-the-ears rabbi from a small *yeshiva* in P'shyskha?

And yet, his hands trembled as he broke the seal on the envelope and read the words within. His face revealed the shock that struck him like lightning. It was an acceptance letter! And it was accompanied by a grand check to cover his expenses! He was to sail to the New World and travel in style to his new congregation. They had sent him $100 American dollars. (He didn't know what a dollar was, but figured it must be a great fortune.) He could afford to bring his small library of books, a new suit, and he might even be able to purchase a proper *shtrimel!***

Nevertheless, he contained his excitement as a good P'shyskha *Yid* should, trying not to beam with delight in front of his students. He calmly told them what the letter said and then insisted that they go back to their studies. But his young charges could tell that Reb Ya'ir was distracted.

---

* The word *Yid* means 'Jew.' The Yiddish plural is *Yidden*. When stated by a person of the Jewish faith, it is quite an acceptable term. However, it has often been used by non-Jews with derision, and in this context is considered offensive.

** A *shtrimel* is a large fur hat worn by many Hasidic Jews.

Soon the lesson was finished and he ran to his own teacher, Reb Zalman. Reb Zalman was the *rosh yeshiva*, the head of the seminary that had been his home for so many years. Many P'shyskha Hasidim had chosen to follow Reb Menachem Mendel to Kotzk after the passing of the holy Rebbe Simhah Bunem, and some even gave their allegiance to Reb Mordecai Yosef of Ishbitz, but Reb Ya'ir stayed in P'shyskha with his father, Reb Moshe, who helped hold together the little *yeshiva* with his friend and mentor, Reb Zalman. So now that his teaching duties had ended for the day, the young rabbi ran to his teacher, his confidante, and friend, Reb Zalman, who was also a true P'shyskha Rebbe.[*]

Breathless, and yet with some pride, he showed the Rebbe his letter. Reb Zalman smiled at this fall into ego. "My son," he whispered in his hoarse voice: "Do you believe it is due to your past merit that you have received this position? No, it is because no one else would take such a position that you received this acceptance. Your inexperience has hidden this from you, and your ego has so puffed up your chest that I fear your buttons will pop."

Reb Ya'ir looked down in embarrassment, but Reb Zalman only smiled, and with compassion continued: "Yet, *HaShem* clearly has something in store for you on this journey, just as he did with your grandfather *and his journey*. I see that the road will be long, and only *HaShem* knows what you will find along the way. We are told that there are red savages there, and it is a young country that

---

[*] Rebbe is Yiddish for rabbi, but in Hasidism became the title of a Hasidic master.

still fights within itself. Your journey will be a dangerous one, and what will you find journey's end? A small congregation of Jews for whom Jewish life is not very important? This is the journey you must take, the quest that *HaShem* has put before you for your own spiritual growth. No Rebbe can do this for you; it is *your* quest."

As the young rabbi looked down at his tarnished boots with a sufficiently shrunken ego, Reb Zalman laughed: "Good, your *Yetzer HaRah** is now in check. You are about to embark on a journey of self-discovery. No pretention to piety will be of use to you on this journey. Your journey is not for this place called 'San Francisco,' it is a journey to the true Self. As you pack, you must drop the excess baggage that you carry, the baggage of pride and the little self. You must take off all that is not the true Self. Young friend, I ask of you that you pack very carefully. Pack for a journey of clarity, of light. This is a great quest, a path to discover how you will serve the Holy One of Blessing. And remember what the Yid HaKodesh taught us, 'There are no rules in the service of God, and this itself is no rule.'"

Reb Ya'ir was very confused by all of this. First, no one seemed to want this position. His ego had been popped like a paper bag filled with air in one of his student's hands. And yet, his Rebbe seemed to be saying that this was the most important journey of his life. He was very confused. He would have to go and speak with his father. His father always had an answer, or at least a hug for him.

---

* Usually translated 'evil impulse,' but I prefer 'shadow side.'

To his horror, his father flatly announced that he could not go. "It's a long and dangerous journey and you won't find Jews with the right level of observance!" Ya'ir blanched. "What will you do there? Tell me! How can you remain true to the Law?" yelled his father, his face reddening.

Reb Ya'ir stumbled and stammered, but finally said with tears in his eyes: "Father, you have always taught me that we do not serve the *Shulhan Arukh*, the code of Law; that is for the others, those who put a white coat on Esau.[*] We serve *HaKadosh Barkhu*, the Holy One of Being! I have thought long and hard about this journey, about this quest, and I have asked myself many questions. I believe that my questions will be of use to others in their questing, and this journey will also be a quest for meaning.

"Didn't Reb Simhah Bunem always say that 'Every Jew has to believe that there is a treasure in his heart, a hidden fortune, only he doesn't realize it'? Well, I want to be a treasure seeker.

"I'm sorry father, I love you, and I respect you, but this is something that I must do!"

To his surprise, his father smiled and gave him a big, comforting hug. "I would not have thought much of a person whose mind is changed easily by the authority of

---

[*] Rabbi Menahem Mendel of Kotzk said that the *mitnaggdim* (the Jews who opposed the Hasidim) served the *Shulhan Arukh* (the written code of Jewish Law). On the other hand, the true Hasid served God. He was pointing out that people get caught up in obeying the 'Law' and forget about serving God.

others. We P'shyskha Hasidim do not bow to any authority other than that of God!"

It was a tearful goodbye as Reb Ya'ir parted from his father and grandfather. His grandfather gave him a strange staff that he had acquired on his travels. His father gave him a pocket-watch and a knife for kosher slaughtering. The boys in the *yeshiva* waved goodbye as Reb Ya'ir boarded an old cart for the beginning of a long ride toward the seaport of Gdansk in Prussia. There he would board a boat that would take him to the New World.

As he sat in the cart, he remembered stories his grandfather had told him of the Ba'al Shem Tov and how he would sit with his Hasidim in his coach and the coach would cover hundreds of miles in just a moment. "*Oy!* If only a miracle like that could happen for me," he thought to himself and smiled. But the journey was long and bumpy.

When he finally reached the Prussian seaport of Gdansk, he descended from the cart and smacked the travel dust from his frock coat and black pants. He walked to the ticket counter and was shocked at the expense of a ticket to the New World. He would have to be careful with his money. What he had thought a fortune was already dwindling quickly.

The ship seemed huge with many fine looking cabins, but his fare did not cover such finery. He travelled in what was called 'second cabin.' It was crowded, a room shared by four men. There was a wash-stand and a jar of water.

Four beds were crammed together in the small space. Reb Ya'ir felt that this was a terrible place to stay, until one afternoon he caught a whiff of a terrible stench. He followed the smell to the lowest bowels of the ship. This was called 'Steerage.' In this huge room, hundreds of passengers crowded together like cattle. He began walking among the passengers here and brought water to the sick to wash their faces and cool their brows. He sat with families (Jews and non-Jews alike) and listened to their stories, comforting them with the blessing of hope. This seemed to make a difference for them. He would not speak of his own journey; rather he listened to the journeys of the others. And he remembered the words of the holy Yehudi, the great teacher of P'shyskha:

> There are three levels of service. The highest level is that of those who perform good deeds the whole day, and yet, feel that they have not achieved anything. On the second level are those who, though they have not yet done anything, *know* that they have not corrected anything in the world. This is good, for there is still hope that they might correct their ways. However, those on the lowest level, those who are righteous in their own eyes, deceive themselves all their lives; their good deeds will be lost.

So he tried to be of service. He wanted to correct things in the world. Steerage became his world. And he wondered where he fell on the Yehudi's scale. If he was succeeding, then he had reached the highest level of service. But then if he was fooling himself, he was the lowest of the low. "Better," Reb Ya'ir thought to himself, "I will think of myself as someone who has not yet done anything to make the world a better place. I will continue to try, and someday, maybe I will be of service."

One day as he was sitting with a family, he saw a little girl smiling among the squalor. He went to her and shared a small crust of bread. She thanked him shyly and immediately shared it with her mother, father and little brother. There was little more than a crumb apiece, and yet they recited the *brakhah* (blessing) for a meal: "Barukh Attah Adonai, Eloheinu, Melekh HaOlam, HaMotzi Lehem Min HaAretz," and relished the morsel as if it were a feast.

Reb Ya'ir did not know why he was surprised to find *Yidden* (Jews) amongst the passengers. After all, why shouldn't others of his people be on the same trip to America, the land of hope and challenge. Looking at these people in this condition, and yet with such joy, he could not hold his peace anymore. He said to the young father, "I have only given you a crust of bread and you treat it like a princely feast."

The young man smiled, "Oh Rebbe, we sit at your feet and accept *shirayim* (the food distributed by a Hasidic master) from your hand; is that not worthy of celebration?"

The young rabbi blushed and responded: "But I am *not* a Rebbe; nor am I worthy of such feelings and actions. You should reserve that for your *real* Rebbe."

The young man replied with a smile: "On this voyage, *you* are our Rebbe, and there are many of your people here."

Hearing this, Reb Ya'ir realized that he had not been thinking beyond his own limited vision. Now the world of Steerage opened up to him. There were *Yidden* here, and he could serve them like a Rebbe. He realized that these people could easily have sunk into the animal soul, the *Nefesh HaBehamit*, unaware of anything other than their own needs. And yet, this young man and his family taught him the true meaning of Reb Simhah Bunem's teaching:

> All existence, other than human existence, can only comprehend itself. But God created human beings, who contain within themselves the higher and lower worlds, so that they can imagine everything in their souls. That is the essence of humanity, that human beings can understand and imagine something other than themselves.

And so, from then on, Reb Ya'ir held services for the *Yidden* aboard the ship three times a day: *Shaharit, Minhah,* and *Ma'ariv.* Men, and more than a few women, came to *daven* with him morning, afternoon and evening, and his congregation grew.*

---

* To *daven* is to 'pray' with deep intention; this is called *davenen.*

On days of inclement weather, when they could not remain long on deck, they made room for *davenen* in the crowded Steerage. On these days, even travelers of other faiths seemed to take strength from the prayer of the Jews and began their own services. What had been a sense of every-person-for-himself began to change. An air of respect for the worship of the others led to respect *for* the other. Politeness, and even kindness, became the watchword for this society of strangers below decks.

There seemed to be only one small problem, and it was not with the *goyim*, the people of other 'Nations'; It was among the *Yidden*, the *Goy Kadosh*, the 'separate nation.'* They could not understand why Reb Ya'ir took so long in his preparations for prayer. Sometimes he even began services late! This shocked some of the more conventional members of this makeshift *shtibl*.** Finally, they came to their Rebbe and asked him what his preparations entailed and why it took him so long to make himself ready for *davenen*.

Reb Ya'ir blushed: "Well, I need to look into my motives. I need to ask myself, 'Why am I praying?' And then I have to make little adjustments, like the navigator of this

---

* The word, *goy*, literally 'nation,' usually refers to a non-Jew. *Goyim* is the plural. Jews are referred to as *Goy Kadosh*, a 'holy nation.'

** It is said that the rebbes of P'shyskha would take their time before prayer to put themselves into the correct frame of mind, heart and spirit. This meant looking inward toward their motive for prayer and directing themselves into a quiet but deep *kavanah* (intention). This sometimes made their services late, according to the halakhic (legal) time for prayer, but this was of little concern to them; for when they did begin, the intensity was powerful.

ship. I need to look at my inner map and adjust my course before I begin my conversation with *HaShem*. That is why, when I do pray, I can pray with total abandon, with ecstasy, and why I move so much when I *daven* and sing so loudly, shouting to God a new song."

When he was finished speaking, he looked down. When he looked up again, the people were smiling. One said: "Maybe that is the fire that I see in your face when you *daven*. Rebbe, your way is different, but your *davenen* seems so pure!"

From then on, those who needed to, started on time; and those who wanted to try the way of the Rebbe from P'shyskha, meditated before *davenen* with the Rebbe. But no matter how they practiced, the spirit of acceptance flowed through the bowels of the ship, giving an inner light to these people.

One day, after *davenen* was finished, Reb Ya'ir listened as a family spoke of their hopes and dreams for the future, and also of their fears. They spoke of their trepidation, the feeling that the world was either opening up for them, or too large for them to survive in. They went from elation to depression. Hearing this, Reb Ya'ir reached into his pockets and pulled out two pieces of paper, one from each pocket. On one was written: "The world was created only for me!" On the other was written: "I am but dust and ashes!" Then, in his most unusual calligraphy, the Rebbe wrote on scraps of paper the same two sentences for the head of the family and said: "This is a teaching of our holy master, Reb Simhah Bunem. When you find that you are overjoyed, read 'I am but dust and ashes!' And when you are overcome with fear, read 'The world was created only for me!'"

From that day on, the Rebbe had many calls for these two phrases. One day, even a Christian minister who was also serving the people in Steerage came to him and asked for the "twin papers," as he called them.

The Rebbe was so busy that the time on the ship seemed to pass quickly. Soon, the three-week crossing was finished and, as he disembarked, he watched his little congregation disappear, swallowed up by the port city of Savannah, Georgia. Then he looked West, and all alone began his long journey on foot.

The Unexpected Guest

IT WAS ALREADY AFTERNOON and Reb Ya'ir was becoming concerned. He had to find shelter soon in order to set up camp. This was not like other days when he could walk until early evening and throw together a quick campsite. No, tonight was special, and he had to prepare for it in a special way.

It hadn't been that long ago—though it seemed like a lifetime—since he had gotten off the ship from Europe that had deposited him safely in Savannah, Georgia.

He had taken buggies and carts and walked for miles to get to his destination—"California." He didn't actually know how far it was from Georgia to his new pulpit in San Francisco; but really, "How far could it be? After all, hadn't many of the great *tzaddikim* (wise and righteous rabbis)—like Reb Elimelekh and his brother Zushya—walked the length and breath of Poland and the Ukraine? Was this country bigger than that?" A few weeks of walking and getting rides on hay and work wagons, he figured, and he was sure he would reach his destination.

He didn't realize that America was not only larger than his home country of Poland, but larger even than all of Europe! Nor did he know then that it was not his destiny to arrive in California for many years. There was so much that he didn't know about this country. And there was always another lesson right around the bend.

In fact, just as he was turning a bend in the path, he almost missed it; tucked away in the brush against the side of the rock face, just off the trail, he saw it. Something drew his attention there. He chuckled as he thought of how Moses had also turned off the trail, noticing something that would change his life.

The rabbi moved the brush aside and slipped into a cool dark cave. "Yes," he thought, "this will be perfect."

He cut some branches from a bush (one that had not been "burning") and swept out the inside of his new home—at least for the evening and the next day. Then he laid out his meager possessions, which included two stubby white candles and a small flask of wine. There was also a small *hallah* roll that he had baked himself at the home of a kind family who took him in for a couple of days, allowing him free rein in their kitchen. Using his own modest implements, he had baked his tiny *hallah* and cooked a chicken he had prepared himself in the kosher manner. He smiled as he remembered the way the children had gawked at him when he was baking the *hallah* and cutting up the chicken. He recalled, gratefully, how one of the servants showed him how to dry the chicken and soak it in salt (which he would have done anyway) so that it would last longer.

Now, sitting in his temporary home, he thought, if only he could find some wild vegetables to add to his potatoes and the dried chicken, he would have a wonderful feast for

Erev Shabbat—the evening of the Sabbath—for which he was preparing.

So he left his cave, his home for the next two days, to search for wood for his fire, and for anything else he might add to his soup pot. He picked a green here, some sassafras there, while at the same time collecting a bundle of wood in his right arm. Soon he was back in his temporary home, putting his greens, vegetables, potatoes, and some of his chicken in a pot of water that would shortly become chicken soup. He had gathered the kindling (little pieces of dried wood and leaves) together, and had taken out his flint and steel and struck them, aiming the sparks at the charred pieces of cloth and bits of fine dried grass in his tinderbox. When he got a spark, he blew on it gently until a tiny flame sprung from the dried material. Next he slid it under the pile of dried wood and leaves and continued to blow gently until the kindling caught fire. He added larger pieces of wood until he had a nice flame going. Next he placed some pieces of wood near the fire in a precarious position, so that when the wood in the middle of the fire burned down, the next pieces would fall in and his fire would last well into the night without the need for him to touch it at all. In this way, he would not "create" fire on *Shabbat*.

In the morning, after eating some of the still warm leftover soup and *hallah*, he would say his morning prayers and spend the day walking in the woods communing with God. Then, home again for a little something to eat before the sunset. And when the Sun had set and he could see stars in the sky, he would light his braided candle, pull out the spices he always carried with him and some more of his dwindling quantity of wine and make *havdalah*, the ceremony separating the *Shabbat* from the rest of the week. Then he could be on his way again, spiritually and physically refreshed.

The rabbi let his mind wander for a moment, remembering so many *Shabbatot* from his youth, warm memories of his mother's kitchen and the hurrying to prepare for *Shabbat*, the smells of *hallah* baking and chickens roasting. He remembered walking to the synagogue with his father, his own small hand clutching his father's large hand. Now that he was so far from home, it brought a smile to his face and tears to his eyes.

But what was that sound that kept intruding on his reverie? His mind reluctantly returned to the moment, dragged back by some sound in the deep recesses of the cave. As he looked back by the light of the fire, he jumped up with shock! There, reflected by the flames of the fire, were two eyes staring at him . . . and then a voice!

"Please *suh*," the voice said with a deep accent he had come to associate with the American South, "Don't *tuhn* me in. I *cain't* go back, I just *cain't*."

He realized that whoever belonged to the voice was as afraid of him as he was of the hidden and unbidden guest. Slowly, the eyes moved forward into the light. It was a young black-skinned man! He had seen them on the plantations and farms that he had passed on the road, and had been told that they were slaves, brought over from

Africa to work for the people in the South. But he had never seen one up close.

The man repeated his plea to the rabbi: "Please, don't *tuhn* me in to the sheriff. I *cain't* be a slave no *mo'*! I got to get *No'th* and be free."

The rabbi recovered from his shock and assured the man in his own thickly accented English that he had nothing to do with the sheriff and was not going to turn him in. Both men seemed to relax a little. Then the black man came up to the fire, noticeably smelling the soup simmering on the flame. The rabbi asked, "Are you hungry?"

The runaway slave responded, "I ain't *et* in two days."

The rabbi replied, "Then won't you be my guest for *Shabbat?*"

The runaway slave said, "I don't know what '*Shabbat*' is, but if it's *dinnuh*, I *shuh'ly* would like some." And with that he reached for the *hallah*, but the rabbi stopped him with a simple gesture.

"Please sir," the rabbi asked, "Wait a few more minutes and then we shall eat. There is yet another ingredient we have to add to the food to make it extra special."

"*Whut's* that?" asked the former slave and now guest.

"*Brakhot!*" exclaimed the rabbi with a smile—"Blessings."

Reb Ya'ir's guest smiled and remembered that this was the way things ought to be. He told the rabbi of the stories he had been told by older slaves about their homeland,

and a few that he remembered from his own childhood, before the slave ship had come and carried him away. He talked about giving thanks for the food that they caught. He told him of the songs they sang around fires just like this one. But when the rabbi asked if he remembered any, he sadly admitted that he could not. The years of the pain and anguish had erased many of the beautiful memories of his homeland. The rabbi's guest became melancholy thinking of all that was lost from his childhood.

The rabbi suddenly exclaimed, "Here we are—host and guest—at a lovely dinner party and we do not know each other's names! I am called *Ya-ir* (sounding the name out for his new friend) . . . What is your name?"

The black man responded naturally, "I'm called Elijah." But he was not prepared for the response this name got from the rabbi.

Reb Ya'ir's eyes opened wide and his breath stopped for a moment. Then he laughed and said: "It's an appropriate name. Elijah was a great prophet who we remember on *Shabbat*, and who is always welcome in a Jewish home on *Shabbat*, if he should come."

Elijah answered with a question, "*Whut's* a 'Jewish' home?"

The rabbi did not answer; he was pondering the question in light of his own circumstances.

The soup was bubbling merrily, and the *hallah* was warm on the hot rocks near the fire, so the rabbi poured a little of his wine into a bowl and some more into a cup. He then took the two candle stubs and placed them far back in the cave. He lit them and, closing his eyes, recited the blessing: *"Barukh Attah Adonai, Eloheinu, Melekh HaOlam, Asher Kiddishanu B'Mitzvotav, Vitzivanu L'Hadlik Ner Shel Shabbat."*

He gave a loose translation for his guest: "Oh Holy One of Being, Whose presence fills all Creation, You have made us special through our sacred connection with You, the connection symbolized by the lighting of the candles of spiritual renewal and rest."

Then he came forward and offered the wine to Elijah, his guest. He said another blessing: *"Barukh Attah Adonai, Eloheinu, Melekh HaOlam, Borei Pri HaGafen."*

Again, he offered his own translation to the ancient prayer: "Oh Holy One of Being, Whose presence fills all Creation, thank You for creating nature that brings fruit onto the vine."

They both drank and Elijah seemed to like his wine.

Next the *hallah* was taken up. And again, the rabbi intoned an ancient prayer: *"Barukh Attah Adonai, Eloheinu, Melekh HaOlam HaMotzi Lehem Min Ha'aretz.* Oh Holy One of Being, Whose presence fills all Creation, thank You for teaching us how to bring forth bread from the earth."

Then they ate. They ate some of the *hallah* and the soup and some of the chicken and the potatoes and the greens. And when they had finished, they were not quite full, but they were satisfied.

That night, two men from different parts of the world, from different traditions, shared their stories: one, a story of study and travel; the other, a story of hardship, slavery, and pain. Late into the night they talked and wept and laughed until, in exhaustion, they shared the rabbi's blanket and went to sleep.

In the morning, they woke somewhat embarrassed to find themselves in each other's arms, each dreaming of home and loving parents, far away in both space and time. They ate some of the still warm soup and some *hallah* and chatted a bit. Reb Ya'ir wanted to go out for a walk, but Elijah was afraid. After all, he was a wanted man, and the color of his skin made him look like a 'possession' in the eyes of all who saw him—except for this strange man with the strange name.

As they were discussing what to do, they heard horses approaching. Their reactions were understandably very different. Elijah jumped back into the farthest recesses of the cave, while Reb Ya'ir started for the mouth of the cave to see who might be there.

"SSSHHHH!" Elijah hissed, trying to shush his host and new friend. "Don't let on that we're here!"

But the rabbi wasn't thinking in terms of fear, in terms of being dragged back to slavery, of whips or the chance of being hanged as a runaway slave; he was thinking along the lines of '*Shabbat* guests'; he was thinking of discussions of philosophy and literature, or at least learning more about this strange and wondrous country.

Whatever their respective hopes and fears, men were coming toward the opening of the cave. They were not what the rabbi expected. They were rough men who traded in human flesh. They were bounty hunters who specialized in hunting down runaway slaves. They made their living dashing the hopes of those who were only seeking freedom. They would capture the man or woman, chain them, and throw them over the back of a horse to be brought back for punishment and a life of misery. Reb Ya'ir had seen the *pogroms* of Eastern Europe, the slaughter of innocent men, women, and children, merely because of their religion. He had seen people spat upon and reviled because they worshiped differently. He had seen children torn from the arms of their mothers to be drafted into the army. But out-and-out slavery—he was unaware of such evil. And the cruelty of men who stole the very dreams and aspirations of other men, women, and children for money, this seemed devoid of soul, missing even the basic feelings of humanity. He was shocked at finding yet another type of evil in this otherwise beautiful world.

With these dark thoughts buzzing in his head, the rabbi greeted his rough 'guests.' There were three of them, and he almost chuckled to himself, thinking of the three angelic guests who visited Abraham in the Torah. But these were definitely not angels or messengers from God. They all were armed with rifles and pistols. They called out—"Hello the camp!" and burst in. They knocked over his candlesticks and kicked dirt up into his pot of soup as they began to scour the cave. Quickly the rabbi stopped them in their tracks—not with a gun or by striking them—but with an invitation.

"Gentlemen!" exclaimed the rabbi. "Please join me. I don't have much, but you are welcome to share what I have."

The men were stupefied as the rabbi tore off a piece of his meager supply of bread and offered them some of his lukewarm tea. The men didn't know what to do or say. They began to bluster about runaway slaves, but the rabbi only answered by talking about the slaves in the Bible. They demanded to search the cave, and the rabbi offered to let them, but also begged them to "stay for a while and chat."

One of the men tried to peer into the darker recesses of the cave, but another pulled him back, whispering in disgust: "Let's get *out-a* here before this preacher makes me puke!" Amid peals of harsh laughter, the three bounty hunters stomped out of the cave.

The runaway slave came forward in anger and some residual fear. "What was you *thinkin'!?!?!*"

"I was thinking that they were definitely not the type of men who would like to join us for some spiritual conversation and a cup of tea," said the rabbi as he poured another cup for his terrified guest.

After a cup of tea and some *hallah*, the rabbi's guest was mollified. He began to tell of the horrors of slavery in America, what would later be called "the land of the free."

The rabbi heard stories of old people allowed to die in the fields. He heard of women sold to breed, only to have their toddlers taken from them and sold at auction. He was told of women raped, and of men being forced to work stooped over in the fields for fourteen hours with only a little break for water. He heard about the shacks that were hot in the Summer and cold in the Winter, and always crowded. The slave told of whips and chains and humiliation, and the ever-present death.

After this, silence hung heavy in the cave. Then the rabbi responded with his own memories. He shared stories of pogroms, with men running wild in the streets shouting, "Kill the Jews!" Men who rampaged through the *shtetl* swinging axes and scythes at anyone who hadn't made it into the relative safety of their homes. He told of babies butchered, and remembered how his nephew had been forced into the Russian army and never heard from again. His eyes misted over as he told of the girl to whom he was betrothed, brutally murdered for the crime of being a Jew.

Both men drifted off into silence as they each returned to memories of the harshness that life offers to some. But soon they looked at each other sheepishly and brought themselves back from the sad reveries that tried to drag them down. There was nervous laughter in the cave.

The runaway slave was understandably frightened of leaving the cave in the daylight, so they sought-out topics that would not touch the sadness that both men knew so well. Reb Ya'ir spoke of his religion, and the slave talked of the "slave preachers" that came to the plantation once or twice a year, who encouraged them and taught them to be proud as "all God's *child'en* should." They each spoke of their hopes and dreams: one to be a free man in the North, and the other to have a congregation in California.

When night had fallen, the rabbi pulled out his braided candle, poured a little more wine, and brought out some sweet smelling herbs. He shared the wine after saying the blessing *"Barukh Attah Adonai, Eloheinu, Melekh HaOlam, Borei Pri HaGafen."* And then the rabbi said another blessing—more strange words to his guest, *"Barukh Attah Adonai, Eloheinu, Melekh HaOlam, Borei Minei Bisamim,"* and smelled the spices, sharing them with his guest. The rabbi lit the braided candle and said more of the strange words: *"Barukh Attah Adonai, Eloheinu, Melekh HaOlam, Borei MeOrai HaAish."* Then he held the candle high in the air, lighting up the whole cave. And the next thing the rabbi did was the strangest of all—he again chanted the strange words: *"Barukh Attah Adonai, Eloheinu, Melekh HaOlam, HaMavdeel Bein Kodesh LaHol,"* then he plunged the whole cave into darkness as he dipped the candle into the last of the wine! He explained that this was a symbolic way of showing the end of that magical time called *Shabbat*.

The runway slave was surprised to find tears in his eyes as he nodded his own understanding of the loss of *Shabbat*, the loss of a day of spiritual as well as physical rest, and that magical momentary gift of freedom. His tears were matched by the rabbi's as the black man packed his meager possessions. The rabbi handed his new friend a small package from his own bundle. It was some of the spices that they had just smelled.

"I hope that when you smell this, you will remember your first *Shabbat*," he said.

Then the rabbi's new friend, Elijah, handed him a something in a rag. When he opened it, he saw a piece of twisted leather. When he looked at Elijah quizzically, Elijah replied, "It is the tip of a whip that was used on me. I kept it to remind me that no matter how bad things get, they were worse when I was a slave."

There was a heavy silence in the cave as the two men looked at their gifts, tucked them away in their respective packs, and sat quietly for a moment. Then Elijah got up to leave, and said: "I has to travel in the dark 'til I get No'th!" he said. The rabbi nodded with understanding. The two men embraced and the rabbi was left in the dark of the cave alone. Yet he was not alone. He would carry the bittersweet memory of this *Shabbat* encounter for the rest of his life.

The Shelter of Peace

THERE ARE MANY STORIES OF THE WEST—stories of blood and smoke, of violent men in a violent time—but Reb Ya'ir created another kind of story of the West during his journey. It is a peaceful tale about a time when very different people came together at a very special time.

The story begins at a stagecoach station in the mountains of Colorado. At the station lived the stationmaster, who kept the horses and fed the passengers who stopped there on their way to California. One day, the stage pulled in with only four people aboard. There was the driver of the stagecoach and his helper, a grizzled old mountain man, and they had two passengers. One of the passengers was a stout businessman on his way to open a bank in California. "That's where the gold is; that's where the bank should be," he was fond of saying.

The other passenger on the stagecoach was a bearded gentleman who wore a very small leather cap on his head. He said that the cap was a *'kippah'* and that Jewish people wore them as a sign of respect and love of God. He also said that he was a rabbi heading for California to lead the first congregation in that area of the country.

The stage had arrived late and the passengers had spent the night. They were having breakfast with the driver and his helper the next morning when the stationmaster burst in with bad news. Up ahead on the trail there had been trouble between the Comanche and White Men. As a result, the trail was too dangerous to travel for at least a week.

The stagecoach driver was upset that he was going to be behind schedule, but the old mountain man who was riding 'shotgun' wasn't concerned with the delay at all. It seemed as if time didn't matter to him. The businessman was angry at the "terrible inconvenience of the situation" and the stationmaster was thinking about going hunting to re-supply the station larder with fresh meat. He knew that his farm out back would supply them with all the vegetables that they would need.

But the strangest reaction of all came from the rabbi. He almost seemed to be pleased about the situation. The businessman couldn't understand this attitude and asked the rabbi why he was not bothered by their predicament.

The rabbi answered simply, "I was planning on staying on here a little while anyway."

"Why on earth would you want to stay in this God forsaken place one minute longer than you have to?" exclaimed the businessman.

"Soon it will be Sukkot," was the rabbi's mystifying reply.

"What in tarnation is that?" the grizzled old mountain man asked.

"Sukkot is an ancient Jewish holiday that my people celebrate to remember our past and thank God for the lessons that our past has taught us." He smiled and looked out at the mountainous desert that surrounded them. "You know it happened in a place like this . . ." his voice drifted off as his eyes glazed over. It was as if he were picturing something far away and long ago.

"What happened in a place like this?" asked the stationmaster, already interested in what seemed like a good diversion to pass the time. He knew that time could weigh heavily on a person not used to living in the wilderness.

The rabbi asked, "Have you read the story in the Bible about how the Jews had been slaves in Egypt and God saved us?" Not waiting for a reply, the rabbi continued: "God then sent us out into the wilderness to live for forty years before bringing us to Yisra'el, the land God had promised to us. This holiday commemorates that time in the wilderness and . . . other things," he continued mysteriously.

"Like what?" the mountain man asked. He liked a good story same as the next man and it looked like they were going to be there a spell.

But the rabbi did not answer. He smiled and said, "You know, it would be easier to show you and then to tell you. Let me go up into that bunch of trees way over there." He pointed to a large stand of trees near a rock pool a couple of hundred yards up the side of mountain. "Let me spend the day up there by myself. Then I'll invite you up there to see what I've done."

"It's a long way up to that place, y'know," said the stationmaster. "Maybe you should do what you gotta do a little closer to home here. Remember there are Injuns about."

The rabbi merely smiled, took a small axe and started for the stand of trees.

"Crazy fool," the stationmaster muttered to himself.

"Yeah, but ya gotta admire his grit," replied the grizzled old mountain man, as much to himself as anyone.

They lost sight of the rabbi as he wound his way up the side of the mountain. They did not see him the rest of the day, but they heard the sound of his axe and some strange chanting noises.

"He's working kinda hard for a cityfeller," remarked the stagecoach driver. "No offence intended," he said as the businessman looked up at him from his place at the table.

The businessman smiled and scratched his head. "None taken, my good man. I wouldn't go out there all alone for all the gold in California!"

It wasn't until late in the afternoon that the rabbi returned to the log building that served as the stationmaster's home, inn, and boarding house for passengers who had to stop for the night. The rabbi was disheveled and dirty. He went out back, washed his hands and face and dusted off his clothes. Then he reentered the building.

"What in tarnation have ya been doin' up there all day?" asked the stationmaster.

"Ya sound like ya been choppin' on every tree up there," guffawed the stagecoach driver.

"Station master, would it be possible for us to take supper up there in the stand of trees?" the rabbi asked. "I'll be happy to show you what I've done and explain what must seem to be my very strange behavior!"

"Guess there's no harm in it," answered a very puzzled stationmaster. "What do ya boys say to takin' dinner out under the stars tonight?"

Everyone agreed, their curiosity barely contained, except the businessman. "I do not see any reason to leave the relative comfort of this pathetic little inn. I have no desire to climb a mountain in order to dine in the dirt!"

"Well, you stay here all alone then," said the stagecoach driver, adding with a twinkle in his eye, "And if you see any Injuns, give um our regards!"

That was all the businessman needed to hear. He rose slowly from the table muttering to himself. But when he saw everyone heading for the trail that led up the side of the mountain, he was hot on their heels.

When they finally reached the stand of trees, they were surprised to see a crude three-sided shelter with branches covering most of the top. The top wasn't completely covered—you could still see through the branches up into the sky, but the light was diffused and it seemed cooler in the shelter than out of it.

The rabbi, with the help of the mountain man, built a small cooking fire and went about the process of making dinner for that strange gathering.

And what a strange gathering it was! There was the stagecoach driver in his large cowboy hat and bandanna sitting next to the businessman in his dusty suit and tie. Across from them, sat the stationmaster in his worn jeans and suspenders and farming boots. Near him, yet off to the side a little, sat the mountain man in his buckskins, moccasins and floppy hat. And over by the fire, sat the rabbi working on the food, wearing a long black coat with some fringes hanging out below his soiled white shirt and wearing the small leather cap on his head.

The rabbi cheerfully served his "guests," and as he passed pieces of bread to everyone present, he uttered some words in a language that nobody understood: *"Barukh Attah Adonai, Eloheinu, Melekh HaOlam, Asher Kiddishanu B'Mitzvotav, Vitzivanu, LeShev BaSukkah."* He translated for them: "We praise the Holy One of Being, our Eternal Council who has made us Holy through the Sacred Connections and given us the Sacred connection of residing in a *sukkah.*"

He then took a piece of bread, ripped it into pieces and handed them out to his wide-eyed guests and said quickly: *"Barukh Attah Adonai, Eloheinu, Melekh HaOlam, HaMotzi Lehem Min HaAretz,"* translating: "We praise the Holy One of Being, our Eternal Council who has brought bread from the earth." And with that, they began eating. When they had finished the meal and cleaned up a little, throwing everything into the fire, they sat back in silence and looked through the top of the shelter at the stars, each lost in his own thoughts.

The stationmaster pulled out an old chipped pipe, stuffed it with some tobacco, lit it with a twig from the fire and drew on it until he was satisfied that it was well lit. He looked over at the rabbi and said: "Its clear ta me that yo're some kinda' preacher man. So why don't ya tell us about this here 'Succotash' thing-a-ma-bob ya been talkin' about!"

The rabbi laughed. "Yes, I guess I am a preacher of sorts. I'm a rabbi, which is Hebrew for teacher. I am a Jew; my people trace back to Abraham and Sarah in the Bible. I will be happy to tell you all about this shelter, this *sukkah*." But first, I would like you all to tell me what *you* think about it.

The businessman spoke up immediately: "It is a pretty poor shelter, if you ask me; I would never want to have to live in a place like this."

The stagecoach driver fixed an angry glare at the fat businessman and said: "I've lived in worse! Before I got this job for the stage line, I was so poor I couldn't afford ta eat and stay in a roomin' house both, so I lived in sumpin' pretty near to like this here—what ya call it, a 'suckah'— so's I could eat a meal now an' again."

The rabbi smiled. "My people call it a *'sukkah'* and you're right; it is a poor person's shelter. We build it to remember how bad it was for us once, and that others still suffer in the like. It reminds us to be sensitive to the troubles of others. But the *sukkah* has other meanings as well."

The stationmaster looked up from his pipe and added: "Ya know, it kinda' reminds me of the booth I build come harvest time to give me shade while I'm out harvestin' the crops."

Again the rabbi agreed. "You are right too; it was used by my people, when we were farmers in the land of Yisra'el, more than two thousand years ago, for much the same reason. Sukkot is partially a farmer's festival."

"And what is it to you, sir?" The rabbi was looking directly at the mountain man who had been silently staring into the fire.

"Well, I'll tell ya," drawled the mountain man. "I been livin' in one a these here 'sukkah' thangs most a my life. I keep on the move most of the time and it don't seem to make sense to build nuthin' permanent. So every time I stop someplace fer the night, I just whip one of these tagether. It ain't no fancy hotel, like back East, but it serves me right fine."

The rabbi clapped his hands and laughed saying, "You know, your right too. When God saved my people from slavery in Egypt, we camped out in the Sinai desert for forty years moving from place to place. The *sukkah* reminds us of that time of wandering. In the same way, seeing this *sukkah* reminds you of the ones you have been building ever since you came to the mountains."

"But why da ya still build 'em?" asked the mountain man. "Ya don' need 'em no more. And what were you mumblin' back when we was eatin?"

"I was saying prayers of thanks for all that God has done, including bringing my people out of Egypt, giving us the Torah—that's the first five books of the Bible—and making us a special in our own way. You see, the one thing that you didn't say about the *sukkah* is that it is . . ." the rabbi stopped abruptly. He was looking at the mountain man who was reaching for his old flintlock rifle. A moment later, the stagecoach driver had his "Colt" pistol in his hand, and the stationmaster was snatching his shotgun. Everyone was silent. The businessman was holding his breath and the rabbi did not move.

Then they all heard what the mountain man had heard or sensed before them. They looked up to see an Indian standing next to a painted horse. How long he had been standing there, and why they hadn't seen or heard him before was a mystery to the rabbi.

Nobody moved. They watched as the Indian reached slowly, cautiously into a long bag hanging from a primitive saddle on the horse.

"Shoot him! He's going for a gun!" screamed the businessman.

"Oh hush up," said the mountain man. "That's a 'medicine bag,' sumthin' injuns carry to pray to their 'Great

Spirit.' All he's got in there are some roots and feathers and his 'medicine pipe.'"

"He ain't gonna' hurt ya. He's just gonna talk to his God the way the rabbi did to his," the Station master added, contemptuously.

And low and behold, as the five White Men watched, their weapons lowering, holstering, the Indian warily raised a long pipe from his pouch. It was covered with buckskin and feathers. He put a small amount of tobacco into it and lit it from the fire. Then he blew smoke to the North, South, East, and West, turning as he did this. Next, he blew smoke up to the heavens and then down to the earth. When he had finished, he slowly approached the White Men. The stationmaster motioned him to sit down. The Indian sat and offered his pipe to the rabbi. The rabbi looked at the stationmaster and at a nod from him, the rabbi took a puff and passed it on. Everyone, even the businessman, took a puff. As the pipe was passed around the circle, the smoke seemed to pacify the disparate men sitting around the campfire.

A deep feeling welled up with in the rabbi. The ceremony of the Comanche warrior was so different, and yet so similar to his own, with the *lulav* and *etrog* of Sukkot that the rabbi was moved to share it. The rabbi rose and unwrapped some paper and pulled out what looked to the others to be some leaves and a lemon. The rabbi stood as the Indian had stood. He quietly chanted in that strange language: *"Barukh Attah Adonai, Eloheinu, Melekh HaOlam, Asher Kiddishanu B'Mitzvotav, Vitzivanu, Al*

Nitilat Lulav." He translated for them: "We praise the Holy One of Being, our Eternal Council who has made us Holy through the Sacred Connections and has given us the Sacred connection of lifting the *lulav."* He waved the bundle to the East, the South, the West, and the North. And as the Indian had done, he waved his bundle up in the air and then down towards the earth.

When he sat down, the rabbi answered their questions. "The bundle is called *lulav,"* he explained.* "And this," he lifted the yellow fruit, "is an *etrog*".** We wave them together as a symbol of our awareness of the presence of God everywhere, and in everything. He looked down at the bundle of palm, willow and myrtle, held along with the citron, the *etrog*. Some say these symbolize the human being; others say they symbolize God's name. Either way, it points me to the understanding that we are all one. Our differences are just flavors in the stew." He said this with a bit of embarrassment, feeling that he had gone on too long about his holiday and his feelings. But as he sat down, the Indian took his pipe bag and handed it to the rabbi. It seems that the mountain man had been translating using sign language for the Indian. The rabbi immediately felt the power of the giving. Without a word, he slid his *lulav* and *etrog* into the beaded bag.

---

* *Lulav* is a bundle made up of palm, myrtle and willow leaves that is shaken along with the *etrog* on Sukkot.

** *Etrog* is a citron that is held with the *lulav* and shaken in the four directions, up and down during Sukkot.

The mountain man continued to translate: "Seems that this here Injun has given you a name. It translates as 'the light giver.' The rabbi laughed, turning a little red: "Actually, that is what 'Ya'ir,' my first name means. Ya'ir means 'light giver.' I guess in Hebrew he was calling me HaYa'ir. That touches my heart. Thank him for me, please!"

Then, the rabbi offered the Indian some of his food, which he gratefully accepted.

As everyone began to relax with the warm food and coffee against the chill of the night, the mountain man spoke with the Indian and translated for everyone. It seems that the Indian had been watching the strange behavior of the rabbi and the four White Men. He had seen the rabbi come up and build the *sukkah*. He had heard the rabbi chanting in a strange tongue. He had seen the rabbi leave and return with the others. The Indian had decided that this place had been made sacred by the rabbi and wanted to show his respect.

When the rabbi heard this, his face broke out in a grin from ear to ear. He said: "This Indian is a *hakham*, a wise man. He is absolutely correct. That is what I was about to tell you. The *sukkah* is sacred to us. It is a way in which we remember that we were slaves in Egypt and that God saved us. It is also a way in which we remember Yisra'el, our spiritual homeland. We remember, as farmers bringing the first of our crops to the Temple as a gift of thanksgiving to God. It is also a way to remember that we once had nothing; we were but slaves. Now that we are no longer slaves, we don't want to forget what it was like. We don't want to allow it to happen again, not to us, not to anyone." There was an embarrassed quiet as the White Men reflected on the fact that in this country, one man could own another.

As the mountain man translated, the Indian nodded and said something back to the mountain man. The mountain man laughed and said: "This here Injun says that you are his brother. You have the heart of a spirit-warrior. That's a mighty powerful compliment, rabbi. He says that this land is his spiritual homeland. He wishes other White Men would understand that like you do."

The rabbi saw the pain on the Indian's face and said: "Please thank him for me and tell him that I am honored. I hope that his tribe and mine and yours will always be able to live beside each other in *'shalom'*".

"What in 'Sam Hill' is *'shalom'*?"

"Peace," the rabbi answered softly, looking deeply into the eyes of his new brother. "It just means peace."

The Miracle of Rededication

CAPTURED AND KEPT UNDER GUARD, Reb Ya'ir waited while the council decided his fate. Lost in his thoughts, he had walked right into the middle of an Apsaalooke camp (the people known to the Whites of this area as Crow) as they were preparing for battle. He would have felt stupid about wandering into such a situation if his fear wasn't overriding all his other feelings. There was no hope of escape; even with his experience in the wilderness, he knew he could not escape seasoned warriors in a situation like this, especially in the dead of winter. That their grievances against the Siksika, the Blackfoot were merited, he did not doubt; still, he would rather not become a casualty of a war between tribes.

His only hope seemed to be the medicine man, the shaman who had been intrigued by his *kameyah*, what these people called a 'medicine pouch.'* The shaman was curious about this strange White Man who seemed different than others his tribe had encountered—a White Man dressed much like the trappers who invaded their land to trap beaver and kill buffalo—but who spoke some Arapahoe and seemed fluent in their ways. His people had

---

* *Kameyah* is a Jewish amulet, often with Hebrew letters in mystical forms on or within it.

many grievances against the Whites, but for some reason, this one made a different impression on him. He wanted to know more about their captive before he was put to death, enslaved or—as Reb Ya'ir prayed—freed. The shaman asked about the 'medicine pouch' and the medicine that was sacred to this White Man in their midst. The rabbi felt a thrill of hope as the medicine man asked about the *kameyah*.

The *kameyah* was for him a reminder of the ancient Temple of his people, and of their tribal life together in ancient Yisra'el. He began to describe the holy Temple to the medicine man who listened with awe (and some disbelief) as the rabbi explained the size and beauty of the Temple. But the idea of tribes coming together to join in prayer and to dance and sing on holy days sat well with him.

Unlike many of the young men, he was not in favor of the coming war with the Blackfoot. So, as the rabbi spoke of the Jewish holy days on which the twelve tribes came from near and far to join in celebration, the shaman's own deepest dream of peace among all the tribes was stirred. Reb Ya'ir spoke of the tribes of Yehudah, Binyamin, Naftali, Dan, Gad, Asher, Reuven, Shimon, Yissaskhar, Zevulun, Menasheh-Ephriam, and the tribe of Levi, which had no land, but which was in charge of the holy place called the Temple. Then he hesitated a moment—a plan had begun to form in his mind that might just keep him alive, at least for eight days.

He took a breath and told the medicine man that he understood his pain and disquiet over the coming war, and he also knew a story that might be of help. However, the story would take eight nights to tell and had to be told with the proper ceremony.

The shaman knew that this was likely a ploy to buy time. But he was also touched and intrigued by this strange White Man, and a 'healing story' must be respected, he thought, and to tell it with ceremony is just as it should be.

So Reb Ya'ir told him that he would share the story of a great battle of the tribes, of how it began and how it ended. It would take eight nights to tell the story of his people's war for freedom: each night, another part of the story would be told; and each night a candle should be lit, starting the first night with one candle and ending on the last night with eight lit candles. He explained that there were sacred words to be shared in the ancient language of his people. The shaman sensed that there was something pure about the promised story, and he agreed to hear it with the ceremony the rabbi suggested. Then Reb Ya'ir suggested that the men of the tribe might also want to come and hear the story. Again, the shaman agreed. His intuition told him that it would be good for the young men of the tribe to hear this tale. And they all would enjoy sitting around a warm fire during the cold dark nights of winter, listening to stories, even the stories of this odd White Man.*

The First Night

So it was that all the warriors of the tribe, the elders, the women, and even the youngsters gathered to hear the tale at the request of the medicine man, a man worthy of respect. The rabbi began by lighting two buffalo fat candles. The first he lit from the fire and called it *"shamash."* He explained that *shamash* came from the word for 'Sun,' and meant 'the one who gives aid,' the one who helps others to see clearly. Reb Ya'ir noticed that there were nods from some of the elders of the tribe.

So, with the *shamash* in hand, he offered the ancient words of the sacred language, chanting loudly: *"Barukh Attah Adonai, Eloheinu, Melekh HaOlam, Asher Kiddishanu B'Mitzvotav, Vitzivanu L'Hadlik Ner Hannukhah."* He translated this as: "We bow before the Holy One of Being, our God, Who has given us distinction through sacred connections, and offered this sacred connection of the light of determination."*

There were more nods of approval and even some calls of agreement by the warriors who heard in this prayer, and especially the word "determination," a call to war against

---

* A *tipi* is a conical portable dwelling used by Native Americans who dwelt mostly on the plains (and very comfortable as well).

* Or, "Be praised Holy One of Being, who is our God, our eternal Council who has made us unique through Your commandments, and charged us with lighting the lights of rededication."

their enemies. They also thought of the distinctions that they would win in the coming battles.

Then, Reb Ya'ir offered another prayer: *"Barukh Attah Adonai, Eloheinu, Melekh HaOlam, She'assa Nissim La'avoteinu Ba'ya'mim Ha'hem Baz'man HaZeh."* This he translated as: "We bow before the Holy One of Being, our God, Who made powerful medicine for our ancient ones, in those days, and at this time."

Again, there were nods of approval and some shouts, but this time from the older members of the tribe, men and women who remembered past glories and wonders. Then the rabbi chanted one final blessing after explaining that this blessing was said at all firsts—firsts in life, and firsts of the year. It might be said at the sight of Buffalo before the big fall hunt, or at the berries that come up in the spring, or the birth of children. He chanted: *"Barukh Attah Adonai, Eloheinu, Melekh HaOlam, She'heheyanu VeKi'yamanu VeHigiyanu Lazman HaZeh."* And again, he translated: "We bow before the Holy One of Being, our God, Who gives life and existence, and has allowed us to reach this wondrous time." At this, the warriors were silent, but the elders and mothers quietly nodded, some weeping in anticipation of those who would not see the next buffalo hunt, having lost their lives in the war that would soon befall them.

The rabbi lit the first candle.

Then, Reb Ya'ir began to speak of a time long ago and far away. He spoke of a people conquered and degraded.

He wept as he spoke of unspeakable horrors visited upon his people, on the people of his tribe by another tribe he called the Seleucids. That tribe, which was larger than all the people of the tribes that together were called Yisra'el, had conquered them. The people of Yisra'el had tried to live in peace. They had even paid tribute. They watched as the Seleucids walked their land, ate their food and dishonored their practices; but for years, they had kept the peace. Then the Seleucids began to desecrate their sacred places and their sacred traditions. They slaughtered the holy men and all who practiced the ancient ways of their people.

As Reb Ya'ir told of the horrors of slaughter and desecration and denigration, the warriors shouted out in anger, thinking of the battle that was to come with their enemy the Blackfoot.

Reb Ya'ir said that the people of his tribe knew that it would happen. They could no longer endure the horror. They had not fought when the enemy demanded payment; they had not fought when the enemy had taken their land; they had not fought when the enemy had ridiculed their dress and their beliefs; but when the enemy tried to force them to give up their way of life, they knew that they had to act. When they were told that they had to forsake the old ways, their tribal ways, when the enemy had slaughtered their young for trying to live in the ways of the ancestors, they knew that they had to make war. Again, there were shouts from the warriors of the tribe.

He told of the people meeting and talking of what must be done. At first, the talk was between small groups in whispers, but later, the talk grew. There were councils: people of different tribes came together and connected in this time of need. The rabbi called this first coming together— "*Da'at.*"

He described *Da'at* as meaning, 'the spreading of shared knowledge.' He explained that the great 'Wisdom,' which he called "*Hokhmah*" was given to the people from the Great Spirit. Then they meditated and thought on it and the Wisdom became what he called "*Binah,*" or 'Understanding.' And finally, a point was reached when the Wisdom and Understanding could be expressed in words; and that was the *Da'at*.

The elders of the tribe nodded, understanding the process and the need for thought and prayer before any action could be taken. Many of the elders, the wise ones, could recall such a flow of Wisdom, a flash of insight so profound that no expression or even thought could contain it. Then a wild race had run its course through the mind, pieces of Understanding falling into place until finally, it became something that could be shared at council.

The rabbi was silent. Somehow they all knew that the first night's story had come to an end. The young men, the warriors went away reassured that the war for which they were preparing was good. Why else would the spirits send this strange man to them? Why else had the medicine man, the holy one, given permission for their prisoner to address the tribe and tell his tale and share his way?

The Second Night

The next night the warriors were eager to continue the story. When they all gathered, the rabbi began in the same way he had the night before. He started with the sacred words, words that he called "blessings."

He explained about the *shamash* again, the one who is exalted and raised for service. And again he offered the ancient sacred words in the ancient sacred language. He chanted loudly: *"Barukh Attah Adonai, Eloheinu, Melekh HaOlam, Asher Kiddishanu B'Mitzvotav, Vitzivanu L'Hadlik Ner Hannukhah."* He translated: "We bow before the Holy One of Being, our God, Who has given us distinction through sacred connections, and offered this sacred connection of the light of determination." The warriors were once again bolstered in their resolve, hearing in these words a call to war against their enemies.

Then Reb Ya'ir continued with the second prayer: *"Barukh Attah Adonai, Eloheinu, Melekh HaOlam, She'assa Nissim La'avoteinu Ba'ya'mim Ha'hem Baz'man HaZeh."* And again he translated: "We bow before the Holy One of Being, our God, Who made powerful medicine for our ancient ones, in those days, and at this time." And again there were nods of approval and some shouts from the older members of the tribe, as memories of past glories and wonders flowed into the night in the light of the candles. As he recited the blessings, he lit the other candles, speaking of the *shamash* whose light helps others to see clearly. There were more nods, especially from the women of the tribe who related to the *shamash* and the quiet service it rendered. Again, he used the *shamash* to light, but this time he lit two candles.

But expressions changed when Reb Ya'ir spoke of *Hesed*, the 'compassion' he felt, the sadness for the losses that would be shared by the whole tribe of Yisra'el. "*Hesed* has two faces," he explained. "One is the face of joyous parents looking at their children, husbands at their wives and wives at their husbands. But the other face is seen in the wailing of loss. Smiling faces illuminated in the three candles of the second night of Hannukhah became long faces of foreboding. The elders knew that the young go to war carrying visions of glory and honor, but return weighed down with scenes of lost comrades burned into their minds and the wailing of loved ones tearing at their hearts.

The rabbi spoke of families weeping together in anticipation of the long war with the enemy tribe, the Seleucids and the terrible loss that must accompany war. He spoke of the hardships, not only on warriors, but on their families as well. And then the shaman touched his arm, and as he looked around at the people sitting with him, his captors, *his Hesed* reached out to them and theirs to him and he was silent.

This night, the young men did not walk away hooping and hollering in anticipation. This night, many people went to sit with family in quiet compassion.

The Third Night

The next night, the air did not crackle with the same excitement as the tribe gathered to hear more from the man whom the shaman wanted them to hear. They came out of respect, the first night. The second night, they came with a feeling of justification and determination. But this night, they returned subdued and quiet, in contemplation. Again, the ritual of the candles was repeated.

Reb Ya'ir offered the ancient sacred words in the ancient sacred language, chanting loudly: *"Barukh Attah Adonai, Eloheinu, Melekh HaOlam, Asher Kiddishanu B'Mitzvotav, Vitzivanu L'Hadlik Ner Hannukhah."* He translated: "We bow before the Holy One of Being, our God, Who has given us distinction through sacred connections, and offered this sacred connection of the light of determination." But this night, the warriors were quiet, hearing in these same words the same call to war against their enemies, but with different ears.

"The Ya'ir," as some had begun to call him, lifted *shamash*, the helper, the lighter of lights, and lit three other candles. "Ya'ir," the shaman had explained, "means 'the one who shares light.'" The people thought of this now as he lit the candles.

Reb Ya'ir continued with the second prayer: *"Barukh Attah Adonai, Eloheinu, Melekh HaOlam, She'assa Nissim La'avoteinu Ba'ya'mim Ha'hem Baz'man HaZeh."* And he translated: "We bow before the Holy One of Being, our

God, Who made powerful medicine for our ancient ones, in those days, and at this time." But this night, in the quiet, the medicine man felt the words flow through the hearts of his people and heard their silent pleading: "You have made medicine for us in the past, please make powerful medicine for us in our coming war."

But again, the people were surprised by their guest (for few thought of this man as enemy or captive anymore). The rabbi spoke of determination and decision. He spoke of judgment against the enemies of his people. He spoke of power and promise and the forming of strategies and tactics. He spoke of the ways of war of that time, so long ago and so far away. He spoke of large armies attacking in formation against a small group of warriors, who fought with stealth and cunning, using the knowledge of their native land to help them. He spoke of the resolve to stand as a free people in their own land.

He called this the night of "*Gevurah*," and he heard the warriors repeating the word. For though the word was unfamiliar, its meaning was not. The word resonated with conviction and confidence, with faith and force. The medicine man was looking by the light of the four small candles, and saw nods and nudging among the warriors and the war chiefs. He was aware that soon war would be the focus of all discussion in the camp, at least the discussions of the men. The women would be focused on life and loss, the men on strategy and tactics. That night, when the rabbi's tale was told, the men went away buoyed up for the challenge of planning, preparing for war.

The Fourth Night

By the fourth night, everyone knew what to expect from the ceremony of the shaman's friend, "the Ya'ir," though where his story would take them tonight was a mystery. The rabbi lifted *shamash*, the helper, the lighter of lights, with which they were all familiar now, and lit four other candles. Again, he offered the ancient sacred words in the ancient sacred language. He chanted loudly: *"Barukh Attah Adonai, Eloheinu, Melekh HaOlam, Asher Kiddishanu B'Mitzvotav, Vitzivanu L'Hadlik Ner Hannukhah."* And again he translated: "We bow before the Holy One of Being, our God, Who has given us distinction through sacred connections, and offered this sacred connection of the light of determination."

The words in the ancient language seemed to carry weight and meaning that was felt by the people gathered. The strange sounds were becoming familiar. And with that familiarity came a spiritual light that grew as the number of candles grew. The people looked to their medicine man with the dawning of a deeper awareness of his wisdom for conceiving this event.

The Ya'ir then continued with the second prayer: *"Barukh Attah Adonai, Eloheinu, Melekh HaOlam, She'assa Nissim La'avoteinu Ba'ya'mim Ha'hem Baz'man HaZeh."* He translated: "We bow before the Holy One of Being, our God, Who made powerful medicine for our ancient ones, in those days, and at this time." Some of the elders, who had spent hours in discussion with the medicine man on the story of the Ya'ir, felt a joining, a coming together of past and present as they felt the words of this prayer to the Great Spirit wash over them. And again, they reflected on the strange visitor with the name 'light-giver' and the wisdom of their shaman to turn this man into a light-giver to the tribe.

Eagerly now, the people waited for the continuation of the story. The Ya'ir began again with the preparations for war. He spoke of husbands leaving wives, and young men leaving parents, to head for the caves of Judea that lay in the mountains, like the mountains just to the West of the Arapahoe. He told of the long knives being sharpened and staves carved for spears. He did not have to explain the preparation of bows and arrows. For weeks the Arapahoe had been making strong bows and straight arrows for the coming war.

But the Ya'ir balanced his story between the physical preparations and the emotional. He balanced the *Gevurah* of the night before with the *Hesed* of the night before that. And he spoke of the spiritual preparations as well.

He described the prayers for victory, but also the prayers for salvation, and not just the physical saving from the long knives and arrows of the enemies. There were deeper prayers, prayers that this war would not be fought for glory and might, but rather for piety and right. There were prayers of sorrow and of hope, for strength and for compassion. The rabbi called this night the night of *Tif'eret*, the night of 'beauty.'

When he saw puzzled expressions among the warriors, he explained: "*Tif'eret* is the balance of *Gevurah* and *Hesed*, the balance of 'judgment' and 'compassion,' of 'discipline' and 'love,' of the thirst to strike for what is right and the hunger for a return to peace and love." The medicine man and more and more of the elders held small smiles in their hearts, for they knew the depths of this teaching. It was the same teaching that they had offered the young men. They wondered why it was that the stranger's words seemed to have more effect than that of the teachers within the tribe. But they knew that we are often blind and deaf to the wisdom of our own people.

For some of the tribe there was confusion. Both emotions, the desire to make war on the enemy and the love of home and family and tribe, thrashed about in the hearts of the warriors as they went back to the warmth and comfort of their tipis that night.

The Fifth Night

Many of the people came early the next night. They wanted to sit near the fire and hear the words of the shaman's friend. They knew that through this strange man, the medicine man was sharing a deep teaching with them. The rabbi offered the ancient sacred words in the ancient sacred language. He chanted loudly: "*Barukh Attah Adonai, Eloheinu, Melekh HaOlam, Asher Kiddishanu B'Mitzvotav, Vitzivanu L'Hadlik Ner Hannukhah.*" And again he translated: "We bow before the Holy One of Being, our God, Who has given us distinction through sacred connections, and offered this sacred connection of the light of determination."

The words in this strange ancient language seemed to carry more weight with each passing evening. The strange sounds were becoming familiar. And with that familiarity came a spiritual light that grew as the number of candles grew. The people looked to their medicine man with the dawning of a deeper awareness of his wisdom in conceiving this event.

The Ya'ir continued with the second prayer: *"Barukh Attah Adonai, Eloheinu, Melekh HaOlam, She'assa Nissim La'avoteinu Ba'ya'mim Ha'hem Baz'man HaZeh."* And again, he translated: "We bow before the Holy One of Being, our God, Who made powerful medicine for our ancient ones, in those days, and at this time."

By the time that the Ya'ir lifted *shamash,* the helper, the lighter of lights and lit five other candles, everyone was sitting and waiting to find the direction of tonight's passage and passing of the story.

The people who had come to expect the same tellings in the same way were shocked from their reverie tonight. They had been lulled into thinking that this man, this light-giver, was but a sitting teller of stories. But tonight, he leapt up and danced around as he spoke of battle. He called this the night of *Netzah,* of 'victory.' He told of huge animals that towered over the warriors, and who had huge, long knife-like tusks that lifted and cut and threw men to their deaths. He told of warriors hiding in caves by day and stealthily sneaking into the enemy camp at night to attack the larger numbers of invaders. He told of great valor and of great loss. Long into the night, he told of battle after battle, of undaunted courage and unsparing sacrifice; for in both the courage and the sacrifice there was *Netzah*, the making of victory.

The warriors whooped and cheered the stories of honor and heroism. As the story unfolded and the Ya'ir seemed to chant his story, the warriors joined in and led him into their style of dancing. Even some of the elders joined in the dance. The rabbi stressed the power and protection that was felt by warriors fighting for the right to approach the Great Spirit, the Great Mystery, in the traditional ways of their people. He said that though many died in the uneven battle with the strong army of the Seleucids, the people knew that they were fighting for a just cause, for the right of the spirit to be free, and so *Netzah* was theirs.

By the time the story wound to the miraculous victory of the tribes of Yisra'el over the Seleucid enemy, the men were covered in a sheen of sweat, and the Ya'ir, panting in exhaustion, sat down at the feet of the shaman who offered a little water to his guest. The shaman smiled at the tired rabbi, who had been stranger and captive and whispered knowingly, "I am anxious to hear where your story will lead tomorrow night, of what follows this *Netzah* of yours." Then the shaman smiled knowingly as he moved off to his tipi.

Long into the night, the warriors spoke the strange names of Mattityahu, the elder who had challenged all his people to fight for their freedom; of Yehudah, his son, the great warrior who led his small band to victory over the huge enemy tribe called Seleucids. They spoke of the bravery of Yehudah's brother, who sacrificed his life by running under and stabbing an elephant, that huge terrifying war animal of the Seleucids, so that it fell on him, crushing him but saving his fellow warriors. They spoke of the name Maccabee and its meaning 'tomahawk.'* The stories were repeated and repeated until sleep overtook the warriors. But the night was filled with dreams of battle and glory and honor.

The Sixth Night

The Ya'ir strolled beside the shaman to their place in front of the Buffalo fat candles. They sat down together and arranged the candles in a line. Then the Ya'ir lit the *shamash,* the candle of service, and with it, lit six other candles as he recited the blessings. Now, some of the people joined him in pronouncing the strange and ancient sacred words: *"Barukh Attah Adonai, Eloheinu, Melekh HaOlam, Asher Kiddishanu B'Mitzvotav, Vitzivanu L'Hadlik Ner Hannukhah."* But when he translated, "We bow before the Holy One of Being, our God, Who has given us distinction through sacred connections, and offered this sacred connection of the light of determination," the people around the fire were looking deeply into the

---

* The Hebrew, *maccabee* means 'hammer.'

candles, feeling their own meanings for the words; tribal meanings, personal meanings. The strange sounds had become familiar. The many meanings of the prayer resonated in the souls of the men and women sitting in the dark, illuminated by the candles and the small fire in the center of the circle.

The Ya'ir continued with the second prayer: *"Barukh Attah Adonai, Eloheinu, Melekh HaOlam, She'assa Nissim La'avoteinu Ba'ya'mim Ha'hem Baz'man HaZeh."* And again he translated: "We bow before the Holy One of Being, our God, Who made powerful medicine for our ancient ones, in those days, and at this time." And the concept the sacred medicine that flowed through the ancients to that time and place touched this very different people in this very different time and place. And they were ready to listen to the powerful words that were flowing through their strange new brother.

The Ya'ir started with the glory of victory, of a people standing bloodied but unbowed. He called this night the night of *Hod*. He explained that *Hod* meant 'glory.' But he also told them that *Hod* had the meaning also of the awareness, in quiet moments, of *what is* and *what is no longer*. He spoke of the large tribe of Greeks who gave way before the small but fierce tribes of Yisra'el.

Many nodded at the idea, and many heard in the story a good omen for their upcoming war. But again they were led in another direction. For the rabbi then took them over a landscape of death and desolation. He told of mothers who would never again see their children, wives their husbands, children their fathers. He spoke of destruction and devastation. He spoke of love and loss. The mood which was soaring with the elation of victory moments before, now plunged with the growing awareness that the vessel of war, even in victory contained terrible loss. The rabbi spoke not of the songs of glory, but of wailing and weeping. The rabbi sang not of the prowess of men, but a prayer for the dead.

He spoke again, as he had in private with the shaman, of the Temple; but this time he did not speak of the glory of the Temple, but of its destruction. He explained that the Temple was a human-built holy place. This concept seemed more strange than the old, sacred language for lighting the candles that the Ya'ir used. He spoke of how the holy place had been desecrated, how the Seleucid tribe had desecrated and scarred the holy place. Many saw in this part of the story what the Whites were doing to their sacred land. They knew the pain and sorrow that the tribes of Yisra'el must have felt. The rabbi told of councils and sessions of prayer to their God that took the place of cheering and dancing at the victory over the hated enemy of the tribes of Yisra'el. He spoke of Holy Days that had been missed in the war and the desire to re-establish the tribal ways.

On this night, the people left with a feeling of loss. They felt the loss, even though the story had contained a victory over an enemy. It was the feeling of one walking over a field just after the battle, of surveying the death of friend and foe alike. It was a sense of knowing that, even in victory, war was a time of loss. It was a dawning of the awareness that in victory there was no glory. And that emptiness, as the Ya'ir shared, was part of the meaning of the *Hod* of war, the realization that there is no glory in war, only an awareness of being and non-being. Some of the people came away with a sense that this new word *Hod* had more to do with walking sacred paths than with glory in battle.

The Seventh Night

On this night, the people were surprised as they came to the fire circle to see the Ya'ir and the shaman sitting with many bowls and parfleches in front of the Buffalo fat candles.* The bowls and parfleches lay together, arranged with the candles in a line. Then the Ya'ir lit the *shamash*, the candle of service and light, and with it, lit seven other candles. Many of the people joined him in the strange and ancient sacred words of the language that none understood. They chanted loudly: "*Barukh Attah Adonai, Eloheinu, Melekh HaOlam, Asher Kiddishanu B'Mitzvotav, Vitzivanu L'Hadlik Ner Hannukhah.*" The Ya'ir smiled and translated: "We bow before the Holy One of Being, our God, Who has given us distinction through sacred connections, and offered this sacred connection of the light of determination." The people around the fire were looking deeply into the candles, lost in thought as they

---

* Parfleche is a Native American bag usually used for carrying dried meat. They were of hard leather and colorfully designed.

continued the mystical process of discovery, their own meanings filling the words. The sounds—more and more familiar—of the chant gave rise to a myriad of feelings. The many individual meanings of the prayer resonated in the souls of the men and women sitting in the dark, illuminated more and more each night by the candles and the tale being told.

The Ya'ir continued with the second prayer: "*Barukh Attah Adonai, Eloheinu, Melekh HaOlam, She'assa Nissim La'avoteinu Ba'ya'mim Ha'hem Baz'man HaZeh.*" And again, he translated: "We bow before the Holy One of Being, our God, Who made powerful medicine for our ancient ones, in those days, and at this time." And the concept, the sacred medicine that flowed through the ancients to that time and place, flowed through this proud and deeply religious people. Then the people were ready for the next installment of what they felt was a spirit trek.

The Ya'ir spoke of people cleaning, re-storing, re-lighting, and re-building after the horror and loss of the war. He spoke of men and women washing the blood of animals and people from the walls of the Temple, that human-built sacred space. He told of sacred objects that had to be mended and made sacred again. As he spoke—and to the shock of all the people listening—the shaman dropped and shattered a bowl. He then invited members of the tribe to come and repair it as the rabbi told his story. The Ya'ir seemed not to notice what had happened as he continued with his story. But as he continued, those who came forward to help put the bowl back together began to understand why the wise shaman had broken his ancient and sacred bowl. They marveled at the teachings of their shaman and his sacrifice.

Meanwhile, the rabbi spoke of men who had been warriors becoming builders and cleaners and repairers. Women put aside their weeping to sweep and sew and mend. Somehow there was a comfort in repairing, restoring, renewing the sacred place. The people worked day and night to do all that they could. Then they stepped back for the holy servants, the shamans of Yisra'el, those of the tribe of Levi, to find more and process more of the sacred oil for the *Menorah*.

The Ya'ir explained how the *Menorah* had seven branches and held cups of oil that burned with wicks. He depicted it as taller than a person and made of the yellow rock that the White Man treasured so much. He told of how they only found a little oil, but how it seemed to last longer than anyone expected—for eight days!

Then, when the Temple, that sacred space of the tribes of Yisra'el was ready, the people too were ready. The work had cleansed them too. Yes, there was still the pain of loss, but now also was the hope that comes from continuity. Yet even as they celebrated the victory and the renewal of the Temple, there was a nagging feeling in the guts of the elders, those who were called the *hakhamim*, the wise ones. They sat and spoke of the war and the dedication of the Temple, and they decided that the war was not the important thing to remember. There were many wars . . . too many. But dedicating and rededicating the

Temple, the sacred space and themselves seemed a much more worthy moment.

The message began to sink in and the people grasped the profound feeling of dedication. Then the Ya'ir continued: "The word for 'dedication' in my language is *Hannukhah,* and that is what we named this eight day festival." He went on to explain that the seventh night is the night of *Yesod.* He said: "*Yesod* is the sense of bringing-in an experience. It is the balance between the doing, the *Netzah* of something and the being, the *Hod*, of oneness with all life and death. *Yesod,* as expressed in the rededicating of the Temple and the people to their spirit path, the bringing-in, the sinking-in of all that had happened, of all that *was* and *is* and *will be. Yesod* is the culmination of all experience, allowing it to bubble up inside us as spiritual growth."

Many of the young people walked away confused that night. What was this "*Yesod*" of which their new friend spoke? But one young man seemed to understand. As he limped away, there was a glow that some of his friends detected. One of them asked him about it. He explained what he had seen in the story: "Remember when I used to brag about my hunting ability? I would puff up my chest when I came home with meat for our people. And when I went into battle though I was the youngest I felt I was the bravest. This was my life, my path, the warrior's path. And then on that fateful day, it happened. Not in battle did I fall; not to the great Buffalo did I fall. I simply fell when my horse ran into a prairie dog village. It was an ignoble mishap. There was no honor in it.

"For a year I struggled to understand why this happened to me. I went to the shaman; I didn't want to live anymore. But our wise man helped me find my true path. Now, though I am still young, I sit in council with the elders. Some say that I am a Peace Chief.* I don't know if I am worthy of that; but though I cannot walk straight and tall anymore, my sight, my inner-sight, seems to be more straight than it was. My advice has been of some help to my people, and this is the path that I can walk even though my legs are bent and broken. I rededicated my life to my people and I am whole again. I think I understand this *Yesod*-spirit of the *Hannukhah* that *the-stranger-who-has-become-a-friend* shared tonight."

His friends walked off in silence, mulling over what their boyhood friend—now the youngest Peace Chief of the tribe—had shared.

The Eighth Night

The last night had come and the people gathered with great anticipation for the climax of the story that they had been hearing and feeling for seven nights.

The Ya'ir and the shaman were already at their place in front of the Buffalo fat candles when the first people

---

* In many tribes, there were men well-known for the prowess in war. In times of conflict, they tended to be the leaders. But there were also men who were skilled at the more difficult challenge of ending conflict and making peace. These men were called Peace Chiefs.

came to the council. The candles were arranged in a line that was becoming comfortable for the people. As the Ya'ir lit the *shamash*, the candle of service and light, and with it, lit eight other candles, he recited the prayer that so many people could now repeat by heart: *"Barukh Attah Adonai, Eloheinu, Melekh HaOlam, Asher Kiddishanu B'Mitzvotav, Vitzivanu L'Hadlik Ner Hannukhah."* As he had for seven nights previously, he translated: "We bow before the Holy One of Being, our God, Who has given us distinction through sacred connections, and offered this sacred connection of the light of determination." The words had taken on so many different meanings to so many different people, each one understanding according to his or her need. The strange sounds had become familiar. The many meanings of the prayer resonated in the souls of the men and women sitting in the dark, illuminated by the candles and the small fire that held the center of the circle.

The Ya'ir continued with the second prayer: *"Barukh Attah Adonai, Eloheinu, Melekh HaOlam, She'assa Nissim La'avoteinu Ba'ya'mim Ha'hem Baz'man HaZeh."* And again he translated: "We bow before the Holy One of Being, our God, Who made powerful medicine for our ancient ones, in those days, and at this time." Some people actually saw in the night sky or in the flames or in their souls the sacred medicine that flowed through the ancients to that time and place. There was excitement in the air as they waited for the conclusion of the spirit tale being told by the friend of the shaman.

But the rabbi did not go on with his story. He seemed to jump ahead in time. He spoke of another tribe, a tribe called the Romans. He told of the horror and death and destruction caused by that evil tribe. He spoke of families being destroyed, men and women slaughtered. He wept when he spoke of the sacred space, the Temple, being burned and destroyed by them. Then he was silent as the light in his face ebbed, as the joy of the rededication of the sacred space was turned into sorrow over the final destruction of it.

Then the Ya'ir began to speak again. He spoke of a great exile; how his people were forced from their land. He looked up at the people and said: "I am here tonight because of that exile.

"The Siksika, that tribe known as the Blackfoot, have pushed you off part of your sacred land, and you will go to war with them. Maybe you will win, maybe not. But people will die and change will happen. But even if you win, there will come another tribe . . . There is always another tribe. Maybe even the tribe of the Whites. I have seen them, and you will surely lose in a fight with them, as we did with the Romans."

On this last night of the story, the Ya'ir sang songs. The songs were of faith and joy, but many of the people did not understand. Then the shaman called to the young Peace Chief, the man crippled in an accident when thrown from his horse. He asked him, "Why is our friend singing songs of joy?"

There was a long silence, for which the young man was known. Then he answered: "It is because of the Medicine Wheel, the wheel of life. And he sings because in joy and in sorrow we are all part of that Medicine Wheel. His people had their day; it dawned and it set, and yet they are still here to tell the sacred stories. Maybe his tribe will have their day again. But in the memories that are passed on, in the stories that are told, in the sacred traditions that they pass on to others, their day shines brightly. In that there is contentment; in that you will find the power of his tribe; and that is the lesson that we can learn on this final night of his story."

The rabbi, who had heard this, smiled sadly and said: "Thank you for your words; you have spoken well. It is what my people call *Malkhut*, the way of this world."

Not many people slept that night. There were many campfires and many tipis filled with people. The next day, the Ya'ir was packing his gear; for as a friend of the tribe, he was free to come and go as he pleased. People were talking of a council. Maybe this war needed more talk, more thought. As the rabbi bade farewell to his friend and colleague, the shaman, the Peace Chief was gathering people for a council. The shaman smiled slyly at the rabbi, and said: "Your trick worked White Man; you are no longer a captive."

The rabbi smiled and replied: "It worked better than I thought it would; for I have learned from your people that every tribe is different, and yet, needed in the great learning that is life . . . *and I have made a friend."*

The shaman waved as the rabbi rode off to bring into *Yesod,* the wisdom that he had seen in this people of pride and power. They were a people of deep thought and spirit and he would find his lessons from the test of *Malkhut* that they had shared with him. As he rode off, he whispered *"Hannukhah Sameah,* may your dedication give you lasting contentment."

Encircling the Enemy

IT WAS FALL, and the rabbi found himself celebrating Sukkot among new friends, a tribe on the diminished land on which they were allowed to live. It was bittersweet for them, he was sure. They were forced to give up much of their land in order to live in peace. The elders had decided that "land for peace" was the only way that they could deal with the invaders from the East. They had made concessions: there were trails now that cut across their land through which the Whites drove their wagons. And along the trails were forts. Some forts had been allowed in the treaty they had signed, but the newcomers had built more and more forts, encroaching on hunting grounds that the people had used for generations. The rabbi worried that his own little hut, built with four walls and a thatched roof would be viewed as just another encroachment. But these were a generous people and loving, and they had invited him to stay for his eight-day holiday with the strange name—*Sukkot*.

It was not the little thatched hut that bothered the people, but rather, another new fort. It was built in a place that would interfere with the migration of the herds of buffalo, that sacred animal that meant life itself to the people. They had petitioned the White leaders back east to dismantle the fort, but to no avail. The Whites had listened and agreed but the fort remained and the walls had stayed up.

The strangely clad man in the thatched dwelling was actually a diversion from the pain of this new broken promise and many had come to visit him. He had invited them night after night to eat in his *sukkah*-dwelling. He had shared his food as they had shared theirs with him. They had exchanged gifts and watched as he shook his bundle of leaves and branches and the yellow fruit that he would not eat. They had listened to his strange sounding words and felt the depth of meaning in the chanting. Though they did not understand his words, the people understood that they were words of prayer to *Ma'heo'o,* the Great Spirit.

There was dark humor in the difference between this White Man and the others. Though they did not understand his prayer-words, the feelings and power of his intention were clear; yet with the White leaders in the East, they understood the words but no meaning came forth. And there was grumbling among the younger men and women in the tribe about that fort.

Here, in their midst, near their tipis, their temporary portable dwellings, was a man in a flimsy shelter, a man who shared with them and respected them and was welcome. Over there were men behind high walls who shared nothing, who gave nothing, who respected nothing, who took all. And they were not welcome on the land of the 'human beings.' The only question was what to do about it. The old men gave council to bide time and wait. But the young wanted to burn it down, count coup* on the enemy and be done with them.

One night, the rabbi found himself invited to a council meeting. He felt uncomfortable sitting and listening to the words of war, though he understood the feelings of frustration. After many had spoken, one old man asked for the visitor to share his counsel.

The rabbi began slowly with a story of his people and what they called the "Temple." He spoke of a day of requests for deliverance, a day called "Hosha'anah Rabbah." He told of the custom of his people to circle an altar seven times, praying for help in the coming year. They would pray for the rains to fall, and mercy to fall like rain. He spoke of the sacred and eternal relationship that the people had to their land, a land called "Yisra'el."

The members of the council felt good feelings toward a people who recognized that they came from the land and had an integral relationship to it; for that is how they had always lived. The people sitting around the tribal council were polite and did not interrupt, but wondered where this story would lead.

Then the rabbi pointed out that the circling seven times is parallel to the seven times Yehoshua, a war-leader of his people, and his army circled the walled fortress of Yeriho (Jericho) before capturing it.

---

* 'Counting coup' was a way for a warrior to show bravery in battle. It refers to touching the enemy (sometimes with a stick especially made for that purpose called a 'coup stick'). It is interesting to note that in this instance bravery is *not* killing your enemy.

He did not go into the exegesis of comparison. He did not explain that the connection is through the Hebrew word, *Va'esoveva*, "and I will circle," which only appears in two places in Scripture. In *Shir HaShirim* (Song of Songs 3:2), it says, *Akuma Na Va'asoveva Et Ha'ir*, "I will get up and circle the city," which some commentators see as Yeriho. The second place is in *Tehillim* (Psalms 26:6), where it says, *Va'esoveva et mizbehekha, HaShem*, "I will circle your altar, HaShem," which connects circling the *mizbeah*, 'altar,' to circling Yeriho.* The altar was circled seven times on Hosha'anah Rabbah, just as Jericho was circled seven times when the people of Yisra'el struck down its walls.

The rabbi did speak of the connection of Yeriho to the altar, taught by the great Rebbe of Ropshitz.** He spoke of the less practiced custom of blowing the *shofar* seven times during the *Hakafot* or 'circling' on Hosha'anah Rabbah. He explained *shofar* by showing them his own, made from the horn of a buffalo. He told of how, at Yeriho, the people circled the city once a day for six days, and on the seventh day, they circled seven times, while blowing *shofar*, and the blowing and the circling made the city wall fall down.

---

* An altar with four protrusions called 'horns' used for sacrifice. There were basically two altars in Temple times: one was for animal sacrifice as well as the sacrifice that included oil and *matzah* and no meat; the other was an incense altar.

** Rabbi Naftali of Ropshitz (1760-1827), a disciple of Elimelekh of Lizhensk and the Seer of Lublin.

"On Hosha'anah Rabbah," the rabbi said, "there are some who still blow the *shofar* and do the seven *Hakafot* to make the wall between us and the Holy One of Blessing fall down. Maybe this tradition will be of help," he said mysteriously.

The talk went on late into the night. Some spoke of what the rabbi told them. They related the story to the occupiers and war. They felt the pain of encroachment and the need for action. But they disagreed on how to proceed. Some wanted to go to war; others talked of waiting and seeking yet another council with the White leaders.

The rabbi did not stay for the whole council. He wondered what the decision would be—*Would there be bloodshed? Would women cry for lost husbands, sons and fathers?*

The next morning, the rabbi woke to a huge commotion. People were taking down their tipis and preparing to move. The rabbi wondered if they were just going to move on or move to safer ground while they planned for war. The tribe did not move away from the fort. Rather, they moved all of their tipis to the fort, surrounding it. They set up camp around the fort, but no one painted for war. Instead, every day they circled the fort dancing and singing. Every night they invited the soldiers to eat with them and share council fires as their guest had done in his *sukkah*-hut.

The soldiers were confused and suspicious. More than once the rabbi overheard the soldiers saying things like:

"Ya can't trust them redskins." And yet, each evening more soldiers came to share in the feast laid out for them by their Red neighbors. Some even brought their wives and children. The people asked the rabbi to share some of his stories, as they shared stories from their tribe. Even the White soldiers began to share stories of their homes back East. The women would talk too, sharing word-pictures of their hopes for their children, White and Red. And everyday, the dancing and singing surrounded the fort. But no longer did the soldiers point their Sharps rifles at the dancers and singers. Some even waved to members of the tribe as they danced and sang.

The rabbi spoke with an elder of the tribe, asking what they were doing. The old man smiled and said, "You should know, you gave us the idea!" But the rabbi was confused. The old man continued: "You spoke of the 'circlings' of an enemy fort and how it fell. But we did not think it would work with these White Men. And you also spoke of walking around your sacred place seven times too. And we understood something that you said. You told us that the symbol was for the purpose of tearing down walls between you and *Ma'heo'o*. So we thought if the dancing and sharing and feasting would tear down walls between you and your God, maybe if we danced and sang and then invited the intruders to feasts, they would know us and the walls between us would fall away too."

As the rabbi looked around and saw men, women, and children—White and Red—sitting and eating and talking together, he realized the wisdom of this elder and his teachings. He uttered a silent prayer for their success.

The seventh day began as the others had, with singing and dancing. The people danced and sang around the fort seven times; but this time, they also blew horns made from buffalo horn as they had heard from their friend, the rabbi. That night, there was the largest feast of all. Almost every soldier was there, including the commander of the fort. They ate and spoke of peace and learning to live together. There was a different tone among the soldiers, the rabbi noticed. And the soldiers left earlier than usual. Some of the young warriors still wanted to attack the fort, but they were overruled by the elders. "Let us wait for tomorrow," they urged. "Remember our friend's story."

    On the eighth day, one of the peace chiefs went to the fort and entered through the doors that were wide open and, low and behold, the soldiers were packing to leave. The peace chief was a deeply spiritual man, but even he was amazed at all the activity.

    The commander told him that he had sent a telegraph to his superiors telling them of the strange dancing and singing and of the feasts and sharing. The leaders had decided that there was no need for a fort here and so they were moving on. Members of the tribe helped the soldiers and their families pack their goods onto wagons and saw them off with gifts and singing.

    But as soon as the Whites were out of site of the fort, the tribe made a big party of pulling down the walls of a fort that they had named "Yeriho."

Crossed Dreams, Shared Visions

THE DAY WAS BRIGHT as a fall breeze wafted across the desert floor. An eagle floated high above as if looking down on the scene below. Four mountains towered over the desert, one from each of the four directions: North, South, East, and West. From each of the four mountains came strangely dressed dark-skinned men. They seemed to be dancing slowly, yet they were approaching very rapidly. Animals also seemed to be converging on the same spot with the men. There were rabbits and snakes and mountain goats and mountain lions, all moving gently forward, creating a large living circle. The four dancing men stood at the four points of the compass among the animals of the circle. Then, from out of nowhere, appeared a beautiful dark-skinned woman, dressed all in white buckskins. Her beautiful long, straight black hair framed her striking features, made even more distinguished by the white paint that covered her face. She sang in a strange sounding language, yet the meaning was clear. She was singing of the harmony of the earth and all its creatures. She was singing of peace.

Reb Ya'ir awoke with a start. He had come to the wilderness of the southwestern desert to renew the *brit*, the 'covenant' with God on Yom Kippur.* He had been in this region of the United States for over a month, praying and fasting, meditating and preparing for the day of *At-one-ment,* the day of attunement. Yet dreams like the one from which he had just awakened, had troubled him. It was not that the dreams were frightening. On the contrary, they were filled with pleasant feelings and beautiful panoramas. And they always left him with a sense of peace. What was troubling was that he had no frame of reference for such dreams. They didn't make sense.

He had only been in this country for a few years, yet he had seen so much. In this place, he felt akin to his ancestors, who had wandered in the wilderness of Sinai. He felt the growth of his soul in a way that he had never felt while learning and teaching in the *yeshiva* in the Old Country. He had been heading for California, where he was to take-up the first pulpit in that newly admitted state. But *he never arrived.* There were just so many detours along the way. Yet those very detours had become journeys of self-discovery.

And now, here he was in a Sinai-like wilderness on the most sacred and awe-inspiring day of the Jewish year, and his dreams needed to fit the mood and the moment. Yet they were not the dreams of a rabbi—no Torah, no *shofar*

---

* *Brit* is a 'contract' or 'covenant.' It is sometimes used in reference to *brit milah,* (circumcision) as in 'to cut a contract.' It refers to the covenant between God and the Jewish people. It has also been used biblically to express the contract between individuals.

blasts, no *Mashiah*—nothing recognizably Jewish in the dreams.* He knew that the sun-darkened men and the painted woman were natives to the land in which he sojourned; yet he did not recognize the tribal markings or the clothing or the large fan-like wooden headdresses that the men wore. What was this image? And why had *HaShem*** sent it to him at this time?

So he wandered and he wondered; for it had been Reb Ya'ir's habit over the past month to roam about in this desert every day, returning late in the afternoon to prepare his evening meal. He used the time to meditate and pray, and to explore his inner self just as he explored his surroundings. And today, Yom Kippur, the day of atonement, was no exception.

But this day he found himself wandering farther than usual, and became aware that he was climbing one of the hills that surrounded the area he had chosen for a campsite. The climb was getting steeper and steeper, until the rabbi had to use his hands to keep from falling backwards down the ever-increasing incline. Finally, he came to the crest of the hill. He walked through a thicket of Pinion trees and, as he came to a clearing, he stopped suddenly,

---

* Torah is a handwritten vellum scroll containing the five books of Moshe, the first five books of the Bible. *Shofar* is the ram's horn which is blown at sacred times, especially during the High Holydays of Rosh HaShanah and Yom Kippur. *Mashiah* or Messiah means the 'anointed one.' It refers to the hope and dream of a world that has come together in peace and respect and in following a Godly and goodly path.

** *HaShem* means 'the Name' and is a respectful reference to God.

rooted in his tracks. Not ten yards ahead of him was a man dressed like the men in his dream!

He was clearly an Indian, though Reb Ya'ir had never seen anyone dressed quite in that fashion or, more accurately, undressed in that fashion. For the man was only wearing a breechclout covering his loins! Well, he also wore a thick cloth headband that kept his shoulder length black hair from falling in his eyes and tall moccasins with rolled up, pointed toes. But other than that, the man was completely naked.

He was sitting in the middle of a circle that had been etched in the dirt with a stick. He seemed to be asleep, though he was sitting up. He was breathing deeply with his eyes closed. Reb Ya'ir stood there transfixed, not knowing what to do: *Should he leave quietly? Should he greet this apparition? Would he end up in a struggle, as Jacob had with the evening visitor?*

As he was trying to make up his mind, the Indian suddenly opened his eyes, gave a quick start and a short yelp, and stared hard at him! Though neither moved for the longest time. Finally, the Indian spoke—"Are you my spirit guide?"

Reb Ya'ir did not understand, so the Indian repeated his question.

Reb Ya'ir asked—"What is a 'spirit guide'?"

The Indian, began to explain: "I am called Chato. I am a Mescalero Apache. These mountains are sacred to my people. I have come here on a spirit quest."

In response, he said: "I am called Ya'ir, and I have come here to pray and to prepare for this day, which is holy to my people. But what is a 'spirit quest'?"

The Apache looked at this strange White Man, wondering how anyone could not know about such a basic and necessary concept. "A spirit quest," he said, "is a search for meaning, for direction in one's life. My people believe that by going off by ourselves to our sacred place—fasting, praying, and meditating—we will find our spirit guide to help us along the way. Our spirit guide gives us power to do what is right for our people, for our world and for ourselves. So we travel to one of our sacred mountains and fast for days, waiting for a dream or a vision that will point us to our power and point us to the right path for our spirit."

Something was surfacing in the rabbi's soul as he heard these words, and a question bubbled up and burst out in a rush—"What did you see in your dream?"

The Apache was taken aback: *How did this White Man know that the dream had come? Did Usen, the One God of all being, send this pale man, who spoke the White Man's tongue with a funny accent, to be his spirit guide?** With uncertainty, he began to speak of his dream:

"*I saw a land that was like this land, yet different. There were hills and mountains like this sacred place, yet*

---

* *Usen* is the One God as expressed by the Apache people. Though there are a number of spirits, good and bad, there is for the Apache one God, the Source of all Being.

there were stone dwellings on the top of one of the highest hills. They were like the dwellings of the Pueblo people, yet different. They were made of square stones. There was a huge wall around this permanent camp—what the Whites call a 'city.' It was very high. Then I was inside the walls and there was another wall, as high as those surrounding the city. Yet, it was different. So many things were the same yet different. I could not understand what I was seeing. I knew that there was power flowing from Usen through this wall. And many people were standing in front of it. They were chanting and praying to Usen. They looked a little like you, but were dressed in many different ways."

Reb Ya'ir interrupted: "Did some have long black coats and black hats, while others wore colorfully striped robes with wide belts and fur hats?"

"Yes," replied Chato in disbelief. Then he continued his account:

"Then a man appeared, dressed differently than the rest. He wore no hat, save a small leather cap on his head, the kind to which our holy men attach feathers for a headdress. He was wrapped in thin, light colored blankets, and on top he wore a serape with fringes on the corners."

Again, the rabbi could not contain himself: "Did the garment you describe have fringes like these?" he said, holding up his *tzitzit*.*

Chato's eyes opened in disbelief. "Yes!" he exclaimed, "Exactly like that!"

"Please, please go on!" Reb Ya'ir implored him.

Chato continued with no hesitancy now, sure that this strange man would be able to help him with his quest:

"The man with the fringes drew forth a large animal horn and blew into it. The sound that came from it pierced me to my deepest center. Then it transported me to another place, another desert. I was on top of a mountain that I had never seen before. And there, floating above my head, was a scroll made of animal skin wrapped around two poles. Again I heard the sound of that animal horn and I was transported to a strange dwelling place. There were people singing and praying in a language that I did not know and yet understood. I understood that they were asking for harmony and peace in their lives. In a box on the wall I saw the same animal skin scroll, but the people were talking from it and laughing and crying at the same time. Then a feeling of great peace came over me, as the whole world began to flood into the room, through the scroll and into my very being. I opened my eyes and that is when I saw you."

---

* *Tzitzit* are the fringes that are put on the four corners of one's garment, as written in Torah (Numbers 15:38). Later it became a small serape-like garment with the fringes attached to the corners.

Reb Ya'ir came forward into the sacred circle of this Apache warrior and sat down opposite him. He said: "Now I have to ask you the question that you asked me—Are you my spirit guide?" Before Chato could ask what he meant, he continued: "You see, I too am on a spirit quest. I never thought of it in those terms, but that is what I am doing. This is the most sacred day of the year to my people. It is called 'Yom Kippur,' and it is the day that my people stand on the mountaintop and look back upon our past, and forward to the future. We review our Circle of Life, which we call a *brit,* or covenant, and we renew that *brit* for the future. For a month I have been preparing for this day. But during that time, I have had dreams that I have not understood."

Now Chato could not help himself and burst in: "You mean like my dream?"

"No," said Ya'ir, "*Your* dream I understand, but *mine* makes no sense to me."

Chato said, with a slowly growing understanding: "Share your dream with me."

Reb Ya'ir told the Apache about the strange men. He learned that they were part of the beliefs of the Apache. They were called *Gan* dancers or mountain spirits. And the woman painted white was called sensibly enough, "White Painted Woman." The two men spoke throughout the day, sitting in the sacred circle. They began to understand that the dreams were really the same, and that they were looking for the same thing.

That night, the Apache warrior and the rabbi broke their fast together. They each spoke of their people and how they had both been thrown off of their land by oppressive invaders. They shared their spiritual search for oneness with the Holy One of Being.

The next day, they shared their morning meal and prepared to leave each other. They exchanged gifts. The rabbi received a Buffalo horn, which had been hollowed out so that it could be blown like the one in Chato's dream, and Ya'ir gave his new friend a golden *Magen David*, a shield of David.*

As they were packing, Chato noticed the rifle that the Ya'ir carried. At almost the same instant, the Reb Ya'ir noticed the Apache's rifle. They stared at each other for a moment and then at their weapons. The Ya'ir mounted his horse, looked back at Chato and made the sign for peace that he had learned from his new colleague on the path to enlightenment. Chato smiled and whispered the word his new brother had shared with him—"Shalom."

The two men rode off in different directions, each on the path for which he had been searching. Their moment together had pointed to the path that these two different men were seeking. It was the path that enlightened the holy lesson, that differences were created by the Creator as a tool for teaching harmony.

---

* Magen David means 'shield of David.' Of course, David never had a shield with a six-pointed star on it. This is actually one of the youngest signs of the Jewish People. Even so, it is arguably the most recognizable symbol of the Jewish people.

Freedom in the Wilderness

JAIL IS NOT THE PLACE to prepare for Pesah. And the fact that the sheriff had confiscated all the rabbi's belongings didn't make things any easier. He sighed as the bottle of wine he had been saving for Pesah was guzzled right in front of his eyes by the sheriff, who was now lecturing him on political correctness in this small New Mexico town.

"You don't stand up for Apaches 'round here, stranger, even for an old woman."

Reb Ya'ir had decided to stop in this town to complete his preparations for a wilderness *seder*. Instead, he found himself a "guest" in the local lock-up. He had been arrested for stopping several young men from beating up an old Apache woman.

When the lecture was finished, the sheriff escorted the rabbi to the edge of town and told him that he was "free" to go anywhere he wanted, so long as he left town.

Hearing this, Reb Ya'ir answered:

"In other words, since you have taken everything I own, and I am not allowed to stay in town, even overnight, my 'freedom' extends as far I can walk into the desert before I die."

"It'll teach you to mind your own business. We don't like Apaches 'round here; and we don't 'cotton' to people who side with them against 'God-fearing' White folk," the sheriff retorted.

As he looked out on the wilderness to which he had been banished, Reb Ya'ir couldn't help but reflect on the Exodus from Egypt. He could finally understand, and even relate to those Jews who wanted to return to the slavery of Egypt. At least in jail he had gotten two meals a day and a cot with a blanket. But now, he had no choice but to walk out into the desert. He remembered the stories of the Exodus, of entering the wilderness of Sinai, and these tribal memories gave him the courage to go forward on his wilderness journey. After all, hadn't his people, with God's help, found their way in the desert?

After three days of walking in the heat and two nights shivering in the cold, Reb Ya'ir came at dusk upon a small fire set in the brush. He had almost passed it by, but something—some forgotten remembrance—nagged at his soul and drew his attention to this burning brush in the distance.

As he approached it, he saw, sitting in the shadows, not far off, the old woman he had helped in town. Evidently, she had been watching his progress and had set-up a camp to draw the attention of the strange White Man who had been of service to her.

Without a word, she offered him food and water and signaled for him to follow her. She put out the fire and began walking. Reb Ya'ir was in no position to ask where they were heading, and having no other alternative, he decided to follow her. The two walked for hours, and Reb Ya'ir was amazed that the old woman seemed to have no need of food, water or rest. She only stopped when it appeared to her that *he* needed one of these things.

After another long march, they came at last to an Apache camp. Seeing the strange pair, a number of people gathered to see what this White Man was doing in their camp. But after the old woman exchanged a few words with some of the elders, Reb Ya'ir was greeted as guest and invited to stay with them.

Having nowhere else to go and no way of getting there, he decided to accept their invitation and spend some time with this people. Thus, Reb Ya'ir of the tribe of Yisra'el became the guest of the tribe called Apache. Being new to the region, he was unaware that this tribe was feared as the most bloodthirsty in the territory, some said, in the whole West. But the people he met now were a quiet, soft-spoken people. They were kind and loving to their children, generous to their guest, and very friendly, though strangely silent, which was completely foreign to this foreigner, used to the constant chatter and discussions of the *yeshiva*.

Right away, they began to teach him to hunt and to gather in the desert. He watched in wonder as he saw how this gentle people ingeniously managed to live off the barren wasteland. As he saw this, he began to reflect on the wilderness experience of his own people, and how he was actually re-living the frightening experience of entering the stark desert wilderness of Sinai, escaping the hopeless slavery of *Mitzrayim* or Egypt,[*] and finding that he could actually live in the wilderness by the grace of God!

Now he began to see some of God's purpose in taking the Jewish people into the wilderness; and why it was such a sacred and essential stage in the growth of the tribe known as Yisra'el, 'God-warriors.'

These people, living on the edge, were vigorous, with a commanding presence, and yet sensitive and compassionate. They lived the joy of life and appreciated the importance of family and tribal connections. It now seemed a truth to Reb Ya'ir that the desert toughens one to the harsh physical realities of life while also opening the door to the world of the spirit.

As he learned the ways of the wilderness from this tribe, strange thoughts kept entering the rabbi's mind. *Their spirituality is so intense.* He thought. *Their word for HaShem, for God, sounded so strange.* He tried to pronounce the word . . . "Usen." *But their faith is deep and real and devout.*

Their ways were different, to be sure, but to them, his morning ritual of facing East, wearing his *tallit* and *tefillin*, chanting in Hebrew, and weaving back and forth up and down, seemed just as strange . . . and yet not.[**]

---

[*] *Mitzrayim* is Hebrew for Egypt. With a clever play on the spelling, it also means 'narrow place.'

[**] A *tallit* is a Jewish prayer shawl and *tefillin* are leather boxes attached by leather straps to the head and the arm, fulfilling the sacred connection from Torah (Exodus 13:9,16 and Deuteronomy 6:8 and 11:13).

He lived in this way with the tribe for some time, learning from them and sharing his story, and the story of his people with them. After a while, he began to speak of a ritual of great significance called Pesah, and the Apaches asked if they might know the meaning of the ceremony he was going to do, and if he might share it with the tribe.

Whether their request was made out of kindness to him or spiritual curiosity, or a mixture of both, Reb Ya'ir did not know; but he did know that this was where he would celebrate Pesah this year, in the wilderness, with this tribe called "Apache."

Together they would enter the dreamscape of a different wilderness. And in answering their questions—surely more than the traditional four—Reb Ya'ir would learn to look at this long ritual meal called the *Seder* as more than a retelling, more than a reliving. The story would become a connection to the ancient dawn of the Spirit Quest of his people. And through the friendship and teaching of this loving people, Reb Ya'ir would enter the wilderness of his soul to follow the path of that Spirit Quest to his own Mount Sinai, his own confrontation with the Eternal, the Holy One of Being, the God of his ancestors.

There were many days of preparation. The women of the tribe were all eager to help the rabbi with his preparations. They worked on the food and prepared gourd bowls and wicker baskets to hold the items the rabbi requested. Even the men helped by hunting for the feast. Sometimes Reb Ya'ir worked with the women, who giggled at a man doing the work of women, but when he went out hunting with the men, the boys also laughed heartily at his poor attempts to hunt like an Apache.

Finally, the night arrived, and the people gathered for the feast that many have helped to make. They sat in a circle, eyeing the unusual settings around them in wonder. Then the rabbi began . . .

Kadesh

The meal began with Reb Ya'ir chanting the blessing for light as he lit two candles made from the fat of buffalo, melted into simple bowls with wicks made from plant fiber: *"Barukh Attah Adonai, Eloheinu, Melekh HaOlam, Asher Kiddishanu B'Mitzvotav, Vitzivanu L'Hadlik Ner Shel Yom Tov."*

He explained that there is a sacred connection between all who share light together. Some of the people were confused by this idea, but a few of the elders smiled, remembering other councils and council fires where they had learned and shared and grown. They remembered stories told by the light of the fire and happy memories of togetherness. For them, the meaning of this strange man's offering touched home.

Then, as the people gaped, he began the blessing over the *tizwin*, a home brew of the Apache (and other southwestern tribes), manipulating the last words of the blessing to fit the sticky sweet taste of the drink: *"Barukh Attah Adonai, Eloheinu, Melekh HaOlam, Borei Pri*

HaAdamah.* Then he drank the entire bowl down. Everyone followed his example, drinking with him, moved by the eerie chanting of the unfamiliar words.

Reb Ya'ir explained that for his people, the day begins at night! There was some laughter at this, but there was much agreement among the young men when he explained that to celebrate sacred days, his people drink wine. They may not have known what wine was, but they certainly understood the joy that is conveyed by sharing a bowl of *tizwin!*

Urhatz

Reb Ya'ir washed his hands in silence, preparing for the first part of the meal—the greens, a sign of spring and hope. The Apache likewise washed off the dust of long and trying trails. Older boys, wearing the necklace of makeshift tweezers and drinking tubes, wash their hands, but don't allow the water to touch their faces, as is the custom for apprentice warriors.**

Someone asked if there are spirit-words for the washing as there had been for light and drink. Reb Ya'ir explained that in the records of many ancient councils, which he called the *Talmud,* the elders of his tribe

---

* Over wine and the fruit of vines, the blessing ends with *HaGafen,* meaning vine. But when it is for fruit that comes from the ground, or if one is not sure, one says *HaAdamah,* from the earth.

** When Apache boys began their training as warriors, they were given a necklace with tweezers attached for removing facial hair and a tube for drinking. Part of their training involved a period when they would not allow water to touch their lips.

discussed the question of whether there should be two washings or one. In the end, there was a compromise—two washings and one blessing, which would come with the second washing. The people laughed and nodded in agreement with the wisdom of the compromise.

Karpas

The greens, the sign of Springtime, were now shared. Reb Ya'ir explained that, for his people, Springtime is a symbol of hope for the future. Then he noticed an old man who, after hearing the meaning of the greens, began to shed silent tears: *Would the Springtimes of old ever shine and warm his body again? Would there again be a time of hunting and roaming in oneness with the world around him? Did his people have a hopeful future?*

Reb Ya'ir sensed the old man's anguish and angst. He looked deeply into the man's eyes and said, as if to everyone: "As long as we have breath, we have hope. Springtime is the promise of that hope."

The old man almost smiled, as they both tasted the greens that the children, the hope of the tribe, had gathered.

Yahatz

Reb Ya'ir then broke the tortilla-style *matzah* that he had made himself for the whole tribe, and offered the traditional words—"Let all who are hungry come and eat," and he added, "Let all who have tasted slavery join us in a taste of freedom."

People stared at this strange man, feeling an odd comfort that they were both hosts and guests at this uplifting and unusual feast. There was a pride in the fact that they were repaying a debt of honor and taking part in a spirit-meal with this outlandish White Man who seemed to share their values of hospitality. It was their way that no one within the tribe was ever turned away from a meal or had to go without a place to lay their head.

Magid

Now Reb Ya'ir began to tell the story of his sacred day. He spoke of being enslaved . . . *and then saved*. He told the Apache of his people's terrible sadness . . . *and their great hope*. And as he spoke, they were intrigued at how, within the one tale were woven many more. The elders were moved and the young men and women commented at different points in the story. He told them of his people's slavery and oppression, of being forced to build cities for the enemy.

As he spoke of this, there were calls of *"No!"* and *"Usen, help them!"* For everyone sitting in this unusual council had heard the stories of people—even family members—having been stolen by the Mexicans to become slaves in mines far in the South, never seeing their families again.

When the rabbi spoke of the plagues, there were shivers and surreptitious looks at the shaman, who nodded knowingly. They had experienced plagues like the ones the rabbi mentioned, but others seem to have been drawn from the desert itself, and the ancient tales hidden within every rock.

And when the waters of the Sea of Reeds parted and then closed on the Egyptians, there were cheers and whoops from the younger warriors!

Then, as the rabbi told of the four children—the wise one, the wicked one, the simple one and the one who does not even know enough to ask—the parents looked at their children and the elders of the people. Their thoughts floated on the gentle breeze of the evening, as if saying— *Which am I? Which is my son? My daughter?* The leaders also looked around, acknowledging that this tribe also had these four types. They were moved that each child in the story was heard and received an answer, for that is the tribal way.

Then Reb Ya'ir asked to hold the youngest baby in the camp as he shared the four questions. He explained that, in his tradition, the youngest repeats four special questions. Then, the rabbi asked them what their own questions would be to the whole tribe. The people shared their questions, each according to his or her understanding; each poignant and powerful, silly and sad. The questions went on and on. The youngsters asked, "Why can't I go on the hunts and raids?" The elders, "When will the Whites be satisfied with the amount of land that they have taken?" The mothers asked, "Why must there be war?" The warriors asked, "Where can we find honor?" The shaman asked, "Will our traditions and beliefs live long on this land?"

When the questions finally died down, Reb Ya'ir continued. He said that he had no answers, "But, if we all ask these questions with *kavanah*, with 'deep intention,' then the answers will come."

The shaman added, "The spirit quest prepares us for the questions, and warrior training prepares us for the waiting for the answers."

Rahatzah

Again, Reb Ya'ir washed his hands, but this time he recited the words: *"Barukh Attah Adonai, Eloheinu, Melekh HaOlam, Asher Kiddishanu B'Mitzvotav, Vitzivanu Al Nitilat Yadaim."*

His hosts—*his guests*—watched and listened as he explained that the words don't speak of 'washing,' but of 'lifting up the hands.' He admitted that it has always been difficult for him to understand why we talk about lifting our hands and not about washing them.

Everyone looked at the shaman. He smiled and stood wordlessly, washed his hands in the dust at his feet and then lifted his arms heavenward, holding them wide as if to receive a heavenly hug, a supernal blessing. When he sat down again, Reb Ya'ir smiled with new understanding and thanked the Apache holy man. The shaman gave him a quiet smile for all could see that raising the hands was a symbol of the reach beyond the physical, the reaching for hallowed existence; it symbolized the search for the Sacred.

Motzi Matzah

Then Reb Ya'ir offered the *Motzi*, the bread blessing over special tortillas that he had made with great care, and what seemed to the Apache, much ceremony. He held them aloft as he continued with the basic bread blessing: "Barukh Attah Adonai, Eloheinu, Melekh HaOlam, HaMotzi Lehem Min HaAretz."

Then he offered a special blessing for the *matzah*: "Barukh Attah Adonai, Eloheinu, Melekh HaOlam, Asher Kiddishanu B'Mitzvotav, Vitzivanu Al Akhilat Matzah."

"The *matzah*"—the strange, hard tortilla he was holding—"offers us a challenge to become conscious of our place on the earth and our connection to all life and its simple joys and harsh sufferings." He shared that it symbolized slavery and hardship, and not having. At the same time, it also symbolized freedom, the freedom to be on the Spirit Quest, to seek the deep meaning of life. *matzah* speaks to bondage and liberation, to bowed heads and hearts, and at the same time, to the wilderness quest.

Many of the women who made tortillas daily, smiled softly at the consciousness that all things come from the earth. But those who had been 'out on the blanket,' on the Spirit Quest, understood the words and this strange bread in a different way, from the dream realm. All knew of the enjoyment of simple fare. How many times in their harsh existence had the tortilla been all that would fill their bellies? And how many times had it been an addition to the feast when the hunt had gone well?

Maror

Now Reb Ya'ir began to talk of the bitterness of slavery, the pain of pogroms and the hatred for his people. The Apache shared the pain of their fight with the Whites, of the racial hatred and the genocidal attempts on their people. They tasted the bitterness of the *maror*, the bitter herb that the rabbi had brought out, and proclaimed it perfect for this strange feast. They understood the symbolism of the bitterness without further explanation. For a moment, there was silence as each person remembered the bitterness of old and new memories. But soon, laughter shattered the melancholy mood as the older folk noticed the youngsters making faces, trying to disguise their distaste for the *maror*, the bitter herbs!

Koreh

At Reb Ya'ir's direction, everyone made a sandwich of the dry tortillas and the bitter herbs. And for a moment, they were all lost in their own dry and bitter memories of the past and the present. Yet, the elders recognized a power in this ritual which gave them hope for the future. After all, didn't the rabbi—who must have been a shaman among his people—say that the tortilla *(matzah)* is also a symbol of hope?

Shulhan Arukh

Then the meal was served—a true feast. The people looked into the camp fire and saw their past glories with gladness. They listened to the rabbi's stories of the Jewish past and present; and some of the elders joined in with the stories of their own people, the old wounds and the new challenges. They all felt each other's hurt and hope.

Tzafun

Then, the rabbi looked around at the joy and deep connection that these people shared and felt almost at home. He laughed to himself. *How strange this would look to my* yeshiva *students back in Europe!*

He rose to speak. The camp was silent and everyone listened. He told the children that he had hidden a special piece of that flat bread, and whoever found it would be given a reward. He had originally planned to challenge the kids to steal the *Afikomen,* as he called it, which he would then ransom back; but one of the women had prevailed upon him not to encourage the children to steal from the tribe. She didn't like the lesson it taught and was afraid the children would get out of hand.

So the children started running around and yelling, looking around the camp for the piece of flat bread. If the other half had been a symbol of sadness flavored with hope, this piece must certainly be a symbol of laughter and joy. Amidst the din and dust caused by the children running and rummaging around the camp, the parents laughed and talked with each other. Finally, with a huge yelp, the *Afikomen* was found! A gift of knotted ropes, like the ones Reb Ya'ir wore on his curious clothes, were given to the child who found it.

Though it was merely a wrapping of string, the solemnity with which the rabbi had made it and gave it away, imbued it with the power of *Usen*, the One God. All the children agreed, looking at the *tzitzit* with intense interest, that these knotted ropes had great spirit-power. The young girl who found the *Afikomen* proudly hung the fringes on her dress.

Berakh

Reb Ya'ir laughed in joy as he explained that now that the meal was over, and it was time to give thanks to *Usen*. The people smiled at how he had pronounced the name of the One God, whom he called *HaShem*.

He then began to chant. And soon, all were chanting according to the same melody, until finally, the rabbi sang out in his strange tongue: *"Barukh Attah Adonai, Eloheinu, Melekh HaOlam, Hazan' Et' HaKol!"*

Hallel

It had been a long evening and one young brave, his legs cramped from sitting so long, jumped up and began to dance! Some of his friends also affected by the drinking, joined him. Everyone looked from the young men to the strange man—whom they no longer thought of as a White Man—wondering how he would react to this behavior during his sacred ceremony. But those who were shocked at the young men's behavior, were even more shocked to see the rabbi stand up and join them! He began singing again in his "spirit tongue" and danced with joy! The singing he called *Hallel,* 'praise to the One God.'

Soon, others joined in the dancing until, all who still could, were dancing and chanting in joy and thanks for this evening, for the terrifying and wonderful stories, the songs, the food and most of all, for the feelings of power—not power to ride faster or shoot better—but a wonderfully deep power, like the one of which the elders often spoke.

Nirtzah

Finally, when the dancing had ended and the tired people sat down again, sweat beading on their faces and shining on their arms, the camp seemed filled with profound silence after the din of the chanting and dancing. The children fell asleep in their parents' laps, and many noticed the strange, wistful look in the rabbi's face, as he seemed to visit scenes far away. It was a look shared by some of the elders as they looked back on different tribal fires. The rabbi seemed in a trance as his mystic language wafted upward with the flames: *"HaShanah HaBa'ah B'Yerushalyim, HaShanah HaBa'ah B'Ir Shalom.* Next year in a camp filled with peace."

The Days of Awe

BY NOW, PEOPLE THOUGHT he looked more like an Indian than a White Man, much less a rabbi. He had been wandering around the western half of the country for more than three years, following the advice of the Talmud, which says: *Dina D'Malkhuta Dina,* "The way of the land shall be your way."* Thus, he had long since discarded his black coat and pants and wore mostly buckskins. He had let his hair grow to the length of his *peyot,* the sidelocks he had worn all his life as a sign of religious commitment to God. His leather *kippah* now sported an eagle feather, a gift from the Oglala of the Lakota people, called the Sioux by the Whites.** He also wore a large knife on a beaded belt and carried a long Hawkins rifle. *Oy!* If his colleagues at the *yeshiva* in the Old Country could only see him now!

At the time of our story, he was in the northern part of the territory known as Colorado, in the foothills of the mountains, near the pass that wagon trains used to cross that great mountain range. But, of course, none were there

---

* This is a Rabbinic concept that refers to living by the laws and customs of the country in which a Jew resides, but it's a lot more complicated than it sounds.

** *Peyot* refers to a tuft of hair above the sideburns mentioned in Torah (Leviticus 19:27). Traditionally, they are not completely cut off. In some cases they are allowed to grow very long. A *kippah* refers to the head cover worn by Jewish men, also known as a *yarmulka.*

now. Nor was it likely that any would be coming through for at least eight months. It was too late in the season for that. Any wagon that tried to get through after early summer was doomed to be trapped by the snows that cover the pass, and which had already begun to fall in the upper regions of the mountains. The rabbi had heard horror stories of people who had starved to death because they reached the mountains late in the season, and stubbornly refused to turn back.

But "the Ya'ir", as he was sometimes called, had come here for a different reason. At the foothills of this magnificent mountain range, called the Rockies, he had decided to celebrate the *Yamim Noraim*. After all, what better place was there to celebrate the 'Days of Awe' than before these awesome mountains?

And so he had put up a *tipi*, just as he had been taught by "the human beings," the Sutaio (better known to Whites as the Cheyenne), who were native to this wondrous country.[*] He had hunted for food as Nimrod had in the *Torah* and laid-in his stores of corn and flour.[**] He had also found wild vegetables and gathered berries. Some of these he dried to be used during the next few weeks, but some of the berries he mixed with dried Buffalo jerky to make *Pemmican*—another lesson he had learned from the people who, according to their own legends had been given this land by God, and who had lived on it since the time of Creation.

---

[*] The name Sutaio means 'human beings.'

[**] Genesis 10:8-12, and I Chronicles 1:10.

He had learned much listening to the sacred stories of the tribes he had met along his journey. And they too had seemed to like listening to the sacred tales that he told them about his own tribe, the Jewish people.

He was reminiscing about this as he set up his supplies, checking carefully the *shofar* he had made for himself from the horn of a Buffalo, when he heard the raucous sounds of a wagon clattering up the hill towards the pass that was near his *tipi*. He couldn't imagine who would be heading up here at this time of year. He carefully replaced the *shofar* in its bag, an old beaded pipe bag, a gift from some Cheyenne he had met a while back. He pushed the flap to his *tipi* aside and gazed upon a tragedy about to happen.

The mountain men would have called these newcomers from the eastern part of the United States, "pilgrims." They were like so many others who would not give up their dream of a better life in the West, even if it cost them their lives. They knew nothing of this land or its ways . . . or its dangers. The Ya'ir watched as they tried to ignore him and his *tipi* and look for the pass they thought would lead them to the Garden of Eden, but which in reality, would only lead them to a cold death.

With a dark humor, he realized that they were ignoring him, not out of ignorant hatred of his people, the Jewish people, but rather out of an ignorant fear of whom they *thought* he was—an Indian. They were frightened and wanted only to pass him by. But Reb Ya'ir could not sit back passively and watch these poor people pass by his camp, knowing that they were headed for certain death.

He ran alongside their slow moving wagon, passing it easily, until he came to the man walking next to the oxen that pulled the wagon slowly on its way.

As the man looked at him fearfully, the Ya'ir said with a big grin, "When strangers would pass Abraham's tent, he would run out to greet them and offer his hospitality. Once, when he was doing this, he found himself standing before three angels. I'm no Abraham and you don't appear to be angels, but I would still be honored if you would join me for some soup and, if you want, you can camp here for the night!"

The man smiled with relief and said: "Thank you sir, we never expected to meet a Christian in this wilderness!"

The Ya'ir fingered his *tzitzit* unconsciously and replied: "You know, Abraham was not a Christian, and I am of his tribe; but I hope you will accept my hospitality all the same."

There was a moment's embarrassed indecision, but soon the people of the wagon were seated around the Ya'ir's fire, slurping soup and asking questions about the way West.

There were two families, the Robinsons—father, mother and a teenage daughter—and the Smiths—grandmother, father, mother and a son about the same age as the Robinson girl. They were all curious about the pass: *Was it a long pass? Was it difficult to find? How long would it take them to get over it?*

The rabbi answered that it was not all that long a pass, and not hard to find or follow . . . *usually*. Indeed, in the late Spring or early Summer, it would take only a couple of weeks to make it from one side to the other. But, of course, this was not early Summer. It was Fall down here and already getting cold. By the time they got up into the mountains to the pass, the snow would be too deep to get their heavy covered wagon through. They would never make it, he warned. He suggested that they turn back and find some place lower down to settle for the Winter. They could hunt and gather, and even farm for the next eight or nine months. Then, rested and strong, they could make the crossing in the late spring with little trouble.

Sadly, nobody seemed interested in his advice. They had dreams of that Garden of Eden waiting for them on the other side. All they could see were the hardships here and the heaven there. The grass was surely greener on the other side of the mountains.

The Ya'ir tried to dissuade them, saying: "The land on the other side of the mountains is pretty much the same as the land on this side, and there is a desert on the other side as well. And even if it were really the Garden of Eden, you just won't make it. You will die from the cold and hunger. Eden will be there next year."

But there had been trouble brewing between the two families; the Robinson girl and the Smith boy were becoming a little too close. They were always trying to be alone together. Their parents seemed to be always fighting, either one family against the other, or the men against the women. They were all sure that things would be different once they crossed the great divide. On the other side, their problems would magically disappear. Once they reached the other side, everything in their lives would be settled and perfect. All they had to do was make it to the other side.

"Yes," the rabbi said, "We have an adage that goes, *Mishaneh makom, mishaneh mazal.* It means 'A change of place will change one's luck.' And yet, it seems to me that the words can have another message as well."

"What do you mean?" exclaimed Sam Smith, as he scowled at his son holding hands with the Robinson girl, "Words mean what they mean and that's that!"

"Maybe," answered the Ya'ir, "But sometimes, and especially in Hebrew, that special, sacred language, words come to teach us lessons about life and love." He too had noticed how close the Smith boy was with the Robinson girl. "Let me try to explain," he hurried on. "The word *mishaneh* can also refer to 'a year,' and it can mean 'to teach.' While the word *makom* is sometimes used to refer to God. So maybe that old phrase means 'A year of changed fortune can teach us about God in our lives.' It seems pretty fitting, considering that the New Year is coming soon."

"What are you talking about?" exclaimed Alice, the Robinson girl, as her attention was temporarily drawn from Michael Smith. "It won't be New Year for another four months or so!"

"Maybe for you; but for me it will come in another three or four days." The rabbi smiled at their confusion. "For Jews, the New Year begins in the Fall."

Then we should wish you a happy New Year, laughed Michael Smith. "How do you do that in Hebrew?"

"You say, *Shanah Tovah,*" said the rabbi.

"I bet that has another meaning too," said Michael.

"Yes, I always think of that greeting as meaning, 'May the changes that we make in the coming year be for the good.'"

So they talked long into the night. The rabbi trying to convince them of the foolishness of going on, and they steadfastly refusing to listen. In the morning, Mr. Smith and Mr. Robinson were fussing with the wagon and arguing over who would sit up front and who would walk with the team. Their wives were lashing down everything that could be lashed down, while the two young ones walked off to try to find some privacy. Only Grandma Smith stayed with the rabbi.

"When I was growing up," she said, "I was taught that Jews were an evil people of Satan. But I never really met one. Now that I have, I don't know what the fuss was all about." After a moment, she continued: "Thank you for trying to talk some sense into those four fools. If they make it, or more likely, when you go to save them, give them this." She pushed a small package into his hands.

The rabbi said: "Of course I will, but why don't you give it to them yourself?"

"I am old and I will not survive this trip. I believe what you said about the snows and all. I know that you have things to do for your Jewish New Year. I saw that old horn and the blanket with the fringes on the corners. But I hope that you will come after them and bring them back and finish teaching them the lesson you started last night."

And before the rabbi could respond, she turned on her heel and headed for the covered wagon.

It had been days since the Smiths and Robinsons had left. The rabbi was preparing for Rosh HaShanah. He had spent time thinking of all the things that he wanted to change in his life. He had meditated on ways of bettering himself. He had prayed for the strength to keep the promises he was going to utter on Rosh Hashanah. He had gone down to the river with some pieces of bread and tossed them in. As he watched them float downstream, he thought of all the mistakes he had made over the past year and prayed that he had learned from them and would not repeat them.

On the day before Rosh HaShanah, the Ya'ir woke up early to prepare for the *mikvah*, the spirit-bath that many Jews take before special occasions. In this case, he was going to go down to the river to a spot that he had found that was deep enough. And though the water was as cold as ice, he was determined to enter it and say the proper b'rakhah, the blessing. He stepped out from his *tipi* to find the ground covered with snow!*

His thoughts immediately flew to the families in the wagon. If it was snowing down here, it must be terrible up there. What to do? Could he afford to wait the ten days of Yamim Noraim, *until after Yom Kippur to go and rescue that foolish little band?*

He knew the answer even before he asked it. He jumped in the river, dunked three times and said: *"Barukh Attah Adonai, Eloheinu, Melekh HaOlam, Asher Kiddishanu B'Mitzvotav, Vitzivanu Al Tevilah,* I immerse myself in You, Oh Holy One of Being, who has given me holiness through Your Sacred Connections and especially this Sacred Connection of immersion." Then he dried off, put on warm clothes, packed some supplies and hiked up into the mountains.

It took the Ya'ir seven full days to find the wagon and its pitiful cargo. They had burned part of the wagon when they couldn't find suitable dry wood and had used the cover to make a poor shelter from the cold, wind and snow. But it hadn't saved Granny. They had buried her under a pile of snow. They were hungry and too cold to move. The oxen had died, still yoked to the wagon. They were a pitiful sight.

---

* A *b'rakhah* is a blessing offered to God. There are formal blessings that (when read singly) always begin with *Barukh Attah Adonai Eloheinu Melekh HaOlam,* 'We praise You, Lord our God, Ruler of the Universe.' I prefer, 'Eternal Council, an equally acceptable but almost unknown translation]. When done in series, the blessings need not begin in that way but do always end *Barukh Attah Adonai . . .* An informal Blessing is anything you wish to say. The shortest blessing is "Wow!"

Yet the rabbi greeted them cheerily, shouting "Hello the camp! *Shanah Tovah!*" He knew they wouldn't understand, but it didn't matter.

He immediately set about fixing their shelter so that it would actually live up to the name and shelter them from the wind. Then he built a tiny fire, melted some snow and made tea. He cut a haunch off the ox and cooked it for them, putting large cooked pieces into a pot of boiling water. After they had eaten their fill, the Ya'ir showed them all how to break up the wagon and make sleds. While they were doing that, he cut up the rest of the frozen oxen and packed all that he could onto two of the sleds. A third sled was used to carry the body of granny.

Finally, they were ready to move out. They all heaved and pulled the sleds. They made very poor time, but the rabbi didn't seem to mind the short distances they were able to cover each day. Every night, he built a small fire and cooked some of the oxen. He made them take off their shoes and rub their feet. He also made them sleep huddled up one against the other in a big heap under the blankets they had taken from the wagon. When they got lower down, where there were more trees and dead wood around, he even taught them to spread a bed of hot coals under some dirt, spread their blankets on top of the dirt and make a toasty, warm bed.

Finally, they made it back to the rabbi's camp. Together they re-sewed their canvas wagon cover into a small *tipi*. They split up the sleeping arrangements equitably and settled in for the Winter. The rabbi taught them to make bows and arrows, just as he had been taught, and they caught game. They made clothing from the hides, tools from the bones and string and thread from the sinew.

When Spring arrived, the rabbi showed them which berries to gather and what plants to eat. They even found some corn that had survived the winter and planted it. As the anniversary of their coming to this place approached, the families began to have a realization. The Smiths and the Robinsons had survived. More than that, with the rabbi's help, they had thrived!

The families had begun by building two log cabins. They had worked together. And as the love that the boy and girl felt for each other blossomed, a third cabin went up for this new couple, the future of the two families. They even asked the rabbi to bless the union, which he did with joy.

After a year, the crops had come in, the berries and grains had been gathered, and buffalo had been jerked for the Winter. They had made this place their Garden of Eden.

The rabbi felt that it was time to share with them the package that granny had left with him. One evening, before the campfire, he handed the package to Granny's son. There were tears as they looked to where she had been buried near the beginning of the path that had led to her death.

They all looked on as Granny's son opened the package. In it was a bag of dirt and a note, which read:

"Dear son! I am sorry that I don't have more to leave you. But this is very special soil. It comes from the Holy Land. It has been handed down in our family for longer than anyone can remember. Who knows, maybe it comes from the Garden of Eden for which you were always searching. Always remember what that rabbi fellow told you; you don't need to find a special place to change your luck. You make the place special to you. You can even carry it with you. Just let the changes in your life teach you. I love you my son."

There was silence as everyone's thoughts sought meaning in the events of the past year. The two families looked out at the Ya'ir who had walked a little distance away. They looked on as he reached into a long beaded bag and pulled from it a buffalo horn that he called by the strange name, *shofar*. Just before he put it to his lips, he cried out *"Tekiyah!"* and blew a loud blast. Then, *"Teru'ah!"* and blew nine staccato tones. *"Shevarim!"* three short notes. And finally, *"Tekiyah Gedolah!"* one very long blast that seemed not to end, finally fading into the mountains that appeared to grow out of their camp.*

They remembered those words that he had shared with them when first they had met. *Mishaneh makom, mishaneh mazal,* 'A year of changed fortune can teach us about God in our lives.' And in the eerie silence after the last blast of the *shofar,* there was a prayer that floated

---

* *Tekiyah* is one long blast in two notes. *Teruah* is a series of at least nine short blasts. *Shevarim* is three short blasts. *Tekiyah Gedolah* is one very long blast held until the person blowing *shofar* passes out or someone yells "Wow!"

quietly on the wind, "May the changes that we vow this year be for good!"

The Tree of Life

AGAIN, THE YA'IR FOUND HIMSELF among the nomadic people of this strange land. He had long since given up on his original goal of becoming the first rabbi to serve the first Jewish congregation in California. His journey had turned into a 'Vision Quest,' as this tribe in the mountains of the Colorado Territory called it.

He was comfortable with this decision, and even with the hardships that had befallen him; for he had grown from his experiences with these people called "Injuns" by the Whites who were moving West. They were not at all what he had been given to expect. They were not "barbarians," but tribes of loving families. The people with whom he was now dwelling called themselves 'Yuhtas,' which the Whites shortened to Ute. The rabbi wondered again, as he often did, if his own people had once been something like them in ancient times, wanderers, nomads on a Spirit Quest. *Hadn't Abraham and Sarah lived in a tent which was not so different than the tipis used by the Yuhtas? Were their family bonds and traditions so different from those of these people?* Maybe that was why he felt such an affinity to them. They were his teachers no less than the rabbis he had known in Eastern Europe.

Today, he sat comfortably in a *tipi* belonging to the chief of the tribe, whose name was Ouray. They were sharing similar, but slightly different views of the spirit and eating soup, slurping the hot liquid that warmed their insides as the fire in the *tipi* warmed their outer selves. But it was their discussion that warmed their souls, the *ru'ah* within them both.*

As so often happened in the chief's *tipi*, they were interrupted. People came in to share problems . . . some physical, but many spiritual. The Ya'ir was fascinated by the spiritual depth of this people and loved learning from the chief. But, this latest caller touched him in a way that he never would have believed possible.

He came in to share a vision that he had experienced, and to seek the council of the wise man who seemed to see what most did not. He was leery of the strange White Man sitting and talking with the chief. But he could not wait to share his vision and to seek understanding. He waited inside the door flap of the *tipi* for the elder to acknowledge him and ask him to sit by the fire. The rabbi asked his friend if he should leave and allow the young man to have his *'yehidut'*, his private consultation with the Yuhtas 'Rebbe.'**

The chief smiled and replied: "No, please stay my friend. I think you might be helpful in this council!"

The rabbi was confused by this answer, but honored to be allowed to watch his friend in such a session. He sat quietly as the elder invited the young man to sit by the fire

---

* *Ru'ah* is the wind-spirit. It is the human part of the soul that opens one to the spiritual side of the interaction.

** *Yehidut* is a personal audience with a Rebbe, in which the petitioner asks a question, or for help in understanding.

on this cold and windy day. He was fascinated as the chief took a bundle of sweet smelling grasses, touched them to the fire and waved them over the young man who waited with ill concealed impatience. When his friend finished the silent ceremony, the young man spoke. The chief interrupted him periodically and translated for the rabbi. This did not sit well with the impatient young man. But what really took the Ya'ir by surprise was the vision itself. The young man had ridden deep into the mountains, and had sat for two days waiting for a vision. When it came, he did not understand its meaning and so had come to the wise man to receive some insight. But the vision was immediately clear to the Ya'ir, though he was sure that there must be another meaning.

The elder man smiled as he translated:

"My young brother saw a tree, but not like any other. It was a tree that grew downward with the roots veiled in the sky. It was being fed through a hidden source in the firmament, and the young man could sense the flow coming down through the roots to the trunk, and through the trunk to the limbs, and finally to the leaves which seemed to radiate light onto the whole Earth. When he saw it, he leaped into the air trying to grasp one of the branches that seemed always just beyond his reach. Though he could not reach the branches, the light from the tree touched him, warmed him and filled him with a sense of connection."

Again, the chief smiled at his guest and surprised both the young brave and the Ya'ir when he said: "I see that *you* have meaning for my young brother's dream. Would you share it with him?"

The Ya'ir was moved by the vision, but also confused. For a long time he remained silent. Then he asked: "Tomorrow, could some people help me to prepare a feast?"

Now it was the chief who was confused. But he was a wise man and understood the power of patience. He looked knowingly at the young man who had entered with a vision and then at his guest. He said to the young man: "You will help my friend prepare a feast. Do all that he asks of you. When the feast is finished, and everyone's hunger is satisfied, your hunger for the meaning of your dream will also be satisfied."

The young man, a warrior of the tribe was not at all pleased with helping this stranger; but he and all his tribe had respect for the wise elder, the man whose medicine was strong and good. He nodded curtly to the White Man and left.

The next day, the young man had an even greater shock; for the Ya'ir asked him to gather nuts and berries with him and the women of the tribe. His embarrassment grew when his friends laughed and teased him as he awkwardly put on a woman's burden basket and went off with the White Man to do his bidding. His anger was visible as he stomped off after the women. But some of his friends, feeling compassion for his discomfort decided to help him with his task. They reasoned with him that if the chief told him to do it, there must be a purpose. Following after the young man and his friends, came this strange White Man who the elder seemed to like and respect.

All day they worked with the chief's strange friend, gathering the berries and nuts that the Ya'ir requested. They were surprised at the difficulty of their task and had a new respect for the women of the tribe. It seemed that the White Man wanted specific kinds of growth. He wanted nuts that had shells. He wanted fruit that had pits that could not be eaten, and he wanted berries that could be eaten whole. They gathered the fruits and nuts all day long.

In the late afternoon, the rabbi sat with the young warrior, his friends and a growing number of young men and women as they separated the fruits and nuts into three piles. The difference in roles between men and women were fading as they all helped in every aspect of this unusual activity. Then everyone took part in the hunting of meat, gathering of vegetables and the cooking. All helped in the setting up of the area where the apparent feast was going to take place. All helped in sorting the fruits and nuts for the feast as the Ya'ir taught them.

The first pile had inedible seeds or pits in the fruit. The second had inedible skins or shells. And the third pile was entirely edible. Each pile was poured into wooden bowls and laid on a separate skin. There was also a fourth skin on which a bowl was placed that remained empty throughout the procedure. The men were curious, and it was an exercise in patience as they waited for this strange friend of their chief to explain what they were doing, and why there was a hide not being used but laid out as if it was waiting for something. But the Ya'ir did not explain; he simply worked at the separating. Then he asked for help in building a fire in a central area for the celebration. More and more of the young people in the tribe came and began by watching; but soon they were helping, some gathering water, others wood.

Before dark, the rabbi was satisfied with the work, but the questions of the young people who had helped went unanswered and unsatisfied.

After spending some time with the rabbi in private, the chief called the people together for a celebration of the Vision Quest of the young man. The chief asked everyone to listen to the words of his friend, the Ya'ir, the one he called "Light Giver."

The Ya'ir stood up and began to explain. He spoke of four Worlds, the first of which was the world of *Assiyah*, the world of action. The second was *Yetzirah*, the world of formation. The third was *Briyah*, the world of creation. And the last, the highest, was *Atzilut*, the world of emanation. His words painted a picture of these worlds, from *Atzilut* to *Assiyah*, descending stages from the Spirit Realm to the Physical World.

The rabbi then asked for the warrior who had originally come to the chief to share his vision. The young man stood awkwardly before the tribe and told of how he had ridden deep into the mountains and had sat for two days waiting for a vision. When it came, he did not understand its meaning and so had come to the wise chief to receive some insight. Then he began to describe his vision:

"I saw a tree that hung down from the sky. It roots were hidden above the clouds. I felt a flow coming down through the roots to the trunk, and through the trunk to the limbs, and finally to the leaves, from which it seemed to radiate light onto the whole Earth. I leapt into the air, trying to grasp one of the branches, but it always seemed just beyond my reach. And yet, the light touched me, warmed me, and filled me with a sense of connection, connection to the world, and to all our brothers and sisters, the two legged and four legged, even the plants and rocks."

Then the Ya'ir stood up and spoke, as the chief had instructed him: "In honor of my brother's vision, we are having this feast!" People stared at each other hearing such familiar phrases from the stranger, but they all knew that their chief used many things to teach his people. This strange and interesting White must be one of ways in which the chief was sharing his 'medicine' with the people of the tribe.

The Ya'ir spoke of the tree that the young warrior had seen in his vision: "It is the Tree of Life that is watered in the world where *Be He Teiht* (he remembered their name for God) emanates power and goodness, what my people call the realm of *Atzilut*. In *Atzilut*, there is no Matter, only Spirit and the energy that flows from *Be He Teiht*. That Spirit-energy passes through the world of *Briyah*, creation, from nothing to something. The world of *Briyah* is the womb of creation from which all things are born. The two legged and the four leggeds, the rocks and trees all come into being in *Briyah*, as does the sacred wisdom that shines forth from great leaders, such as your chief, my teacher Ouray."

At this, there were nods and shouts of agreement and pleasure that this stranger should know the greatness of their leader. The Ya'ir continued: "That wisdom is given to all—though most of us do not know how to find it in ourselves—we have flashes of it, moments of awareness, gifts from *Be He Teiht*, as you have had," he smiled at the young warrior whose chest puffed up with pride. "Then the Spirit-energy flows into the world of *Yetzirah*, formation, where formless becomes form. Feelings become real, as your feeling of pride is real," the rabbi grinned at the young man who blushed just a little. "And finally, the flow reaches the realm of the physical, this world. It feeds all in the realm of doing, of action, our actions, those of the animals, the trees and grass, even the rocks of the earth. For this is the world of *Assiyah*, of action. All action can be in harmony with the four worlds, but only the action of the two leggeds can harm the world of *Assiyah*, hurt our brothers and sisters, two leggeds and four leggeds, and destroy our Mother, the Earth. The choice is ours.

"This ceremony is to point us towards that harmony. Tonight, we eat fruits and nuts, representing each world. For *Atzilut*, the world of emanation, the completely non-physical aspect of the universe, no fruit is consumed for there is no representation of *Be He Teiht*. For *Briyah*, the world of creation, fruits that have neither inedible pit on

the inside, nor shell on the outside, have been chosen.*
In the Spirit Realm of Creation, all is consumed and yet continues to exist. The world of *Yetzirah*, the world of formation, is signified by fruits that have a pit on the inside, but the outside can be eaten.** The pits serve to remind us of the circle of life, birth, death and rebirth. Finally, *Assiyah*, the world of action, the tangible world, encompasses fruits that have a shell that must be discarded, but the inside may be eaten."***

Feeling more comfortable as he spoke, the Ya'ir, continued: "The Spirit-Guide that I follow is called Torah, and Torah compares the human being to the tree of the field. It so happens that my brother came to the chief on this day that my people call T'u B'Shvat, which is a day of judgment, an occasion for changes and self-searching. In a sacred teaching called *Masehet Yoma*, it says, 'Yah (who you call *Be He Teiht*) saw that the *tzaddikim* (the righteous ones, like grandfather, your chief) are few, and so planted them in each and every generation.' Your chief, it seems to me, is like the tree that my brother saw in his vision." At this, many of the elders nodded and even smiled. "From him comes much light." People were listening more closely now. "*Be He Teiht*, who my people call *Yah*,****

---

* Grapes, fig, apples, citrons, lemons, pears, blueberries, raspberries, quinces, carobs.

** Olives, dates, cherries, jujubes, persimmons, apricots, peaches, loquats, plums, hackberries.

*** Pomegranates, walnuts, almonds, pine nuts, chestnuts, hazelnuts, coconuts, Brazil nuts, pistachios, pecans.

**** The first two letters of God's sacred and ineffable Name.

waters and strengthens the roots of the Tree of Wisdom, the Tree of Life. And from this tree comes the fruit of wisdom."

The flow of light, the flow of wisdom originates in *Atzilut*, the realm of emanation. In that world, there is no separation: all is one. But that is far from our world, the world of *Assiyah*, of action. Tonight, as we feast, the realm of *Atzilut* is represented by the empty blanket, for there is no difference between what is eaten and those who eat. If there is no difference, then we need not eat or be eaten. We do not fight or love or do. We simply are; we are all one, the trees, the two leggeds, the four leggeds, the White and the Red, the rocks and the water, all one without separation.

But the tree that my brother saw was not just roots; it had a trunk, and the trunk is *Briyah*, the world of creation. We can put things together to make tools and weapons, but we cannot make something from nothing; that comes from *Be He Teiht, Yah,* in the world of *Briyah*. When we have visions, like my brother's, we catch a glimpse of the world of *Briyah*. When we stop to feel the wind and sun and rain, we connect to the *Briyah*-flow from *Be He Teiht, Yah,* the source of all. It flows from the roots; it forms the trunk. We represent this with fruits that we can eat in their entirety. Creation, which comes from *Be He Teiht, Yah,* is perfect the way it is; we can enjoy it whole. At this point, the Ya'ir picked up a berry and said some words that no one understood—yet they sensed that the words were sacred. He said: "*Barukh Attah Adonai, Eloheinu, Melekh HaOlam, Borei Pri HaAdamah.*" He translated: "We bend to You, Holy One of Being, our Eternal Council, Who created the fruit of Mother Earth!" At this, he ate the berry, and everyone followed suit, eating from the bowls on the blanket of *Briyah*.

"The branches and leaves of the tree in my brother's dream is the world of *Yetzirah*," continued the Ya'ir. "When beautiful baskets are woven, warm tipis are made, when loving parents give birth to babies, we are part of *Yetzirah*. In the world of *Yetzirah*, seeds become trees, and trees give fruit, their own future hidden within. So too, when the children of this people see parents building, forming, making and loving, the seeds of that sweet fruit are planted for the future, may it always be so. And with that the rabbi repeated the blessing and the people ate the fruits with seeds and then put the seeds aside to be scattered that there might be fruit in this same place when they return next year.

The people seemed to be enjoying the words of the chief's friend, maybe because they were eating the feast prepared by the young warriors and women of the tribe as he was talking, or maybe because the wise and wizened old chief seemed to enjoy them so much—but also because the White Man's words began to bring the young warrior's Vision Quest into focus. But for whatever reason, the people waited anxiously to see how the next world would unfold.

The Ya'ir hesitated. *Assiyah* should be the easiest world to comprehend, but he knew that it would also be the most painful. He began by taking a nut and breaking off the shell. He then threw the shell on the ground. "To walk on this shell would cause pain and suffering," he began. "Yet the fruit within is good for food. My people call the shell *klippah** and we tell a story about it."

A story is always a good thing, and the people were eager to hear one from this man. This man looked like a 'hat man,' a 'White Man,' a stranger, but he spoke like a tribal person. "Oh yes," they whispered sagely one to another, "he is tribal; but certainly not of this tribe" some laughed to themselves, "but tribal."

The Ya'ir began his story:

"When, according to the legends of my people, HaShem (that is another name that we have for *Be He Teiht*) began to create, one of the first things created was light. But this was no ordinary light, not the light that comes from the sun. No, this was an inner light, a special light. Sometimes we see this light when we seek visions, as my brother did. Some people never see this kind of light, and there are others who seem to be bathed in it." At this, he looked respectfully at the chief. "*HaShem* created vessels to carry this special light into our world, the world of *Assiyah*. But the light had been created in *Atzilut*, the world of pure Spirit, and as it traveled through the different worlds of *Briyah* and *Yetzirah*, becoming more tangible, the pressure intensified and the vessel shattered. It left, in the world of *Assiyah*, our world, broken and

---

* Shard; this refers to the negative that exists in this world alongside the light of *HaShem*, God.

sharp shards of vessel, and hidden within was that great light.

"In our lives in the world of *Assiyah*, the world of action, we often cut ourselves on the shards of that vessel. It does not mean that we are bad or wrong; it just means that there are many shards and many feet, and the one cuts the other. But if we are wise, and if we have good teachers," again he looked at the chief, "we may pluck the light from the shards and learn the lessons of this light and use it to light our way. I have come to see you as friends, and I want to repay your hospitality and kindness to me. I have come a long way and seen many things. I have seen few things with a beauty equal to this tribe."

At this, many of the people smiled. "This one," they thought, "has wisdom, even if he looks like the 'hat men' who come searching for the yellow iron."

"But I am afraid, afraid for my new friends. There are shards coming that are very long and sharp. There are shards that gleam in the sun as men wield them from horseback as they come to take what is yours."

Some of the men flashed on sights that they had seen, or of which they had heard; men in blue coats riding horses across the prairie with long gleaming knives raised and dripping blood. It chilled them even in their blankets.

"I wish that it were not so. I wish that there were fewer of them and more of you, but that is not the case. I can only pray that the shards will not harm you greatly, and that you will find the light hidden in the shards. I do not know the answers; I do not have that much light. I only know to warn you of the coming of the long gleaming shards that number more than the buffalo in the season of growth. And I am saddened by it. But even in the sadness of shards in the world of *Assiyah*, I offer a blessing to HaShem, to *Be He Teiht*, for the fruit, the light within the shell. May we learn the lessons, may we see the light, may we eat of the fruit." With that the rabbi crushed a shell in his hand and pulled from it the nut inside, repeated the blessing and ate. But some noticed that the shell had cut his hand, and from it blood dripped on the ground.

The chief now stood up and ate from the bowl of nuts. He drank water and then he spoke: "It is good to hear from wise men of different tribes, to hear their council and to grow wise ourselves. I thank my friend, the Light Giver, for his words. I thank my young brother for bringing his vision to us.

"I wish the Whites had people who knew the ways of the tribe; for if they did, the shards of which my friend speaks would remain sheathed. Maybe that is something that we will be able to teach them. But for now, we will remember the council of our friend." He turned and embraced the rabbi.

That night, the rabbi had a troubled sleep, and he was not alone. Many of the elders and the young warriors stayed up and talked of the future and what they should do. The next morning, the chief met with the rabbi. He told him that the people had made their decisions. First they would move their camp deeper into the mountains. The long shards wanted land for the yellow iron that pleased them so much. They wanted land on which to build. The people would move deeper into the mountains and live in places that the Whites would not want. This would protect them from the long shards. The second part of the decision showed as much courage as the first had understanding. Chief Ouray would council with the Whites. This was the light that they had discovered during the long night's council. He knew that the tribe would have to give up much. But he also knew the dangers of the *klippot* of which the Ya'ir had spoken. Chief Ouray was a man who had tasted the fruit within the *klippot*. He was a man who had found light among the *klippot,* and he courageously chose to seek a path for his people among the shards.

The Ya'ir was sad to say goodbye to his friends. They exchanged gifts, the Ya'ir giving a tiny scroll with strange writing to the chief, the chief giving a small pouch with four wraps inside: one holding seeds, another shells, a third with dried fruit, and the last an empty wrap. The Ya'ir was moved to tears at the gift. Soon the Ya'ir was astride his horse and on his way and the tribe known as the Ute was disappearing into the mountains of the land called Colorado.

Afterword

By 1861, the greed for gold attracted prospectors by the hundreds to invade the high country of Colorado. All along the mountains, picks and shovels attacked the earth.

From Boulder, on the Front Range, to the San Juan Mountains over the Continental Divide, gold seekers stumbled and trampled the earth. The government tried to keep prospectors away from the San Juan country, but was unsuccessful.

The San Juan country was Yuhtas Indian country. When the miners invaded their land, the Yuhtas tried with words to stop the invasion and destruction of their land.

An Uncompahgre chief, Ouray, became the Peace Chief who sought peace with and justice from the White Men. Chief Ouray, the Yuhtas name meaning "arrow," had dealt with the White Men for years. He sought peace and security for his people upon their land.

Ouray was a wise man who had spent time with other tribes and in contact with non-Native Americans. He was raised in his mother's tribe (the Apache), although his father was a Ute. His childhood was spent near Taos, New Mexico. He attended Catholic services and mastered the Spanish and English languages. His knowledge of English, Spanish, Yuhtas and Apache, and his knowledge of the different ways in which these people viewed the land prepared him for his later encounters. His intellect would impress the great White leaders of Washington D.C., as well as his own people.

Ouray married a Tabequache Yuhtas maiden by the name of Chipeta in 1859. Chipeta was a Kiowa Apache adopted by the Utes as a child. She was a wise and brave woman who lived a traditional tribal life.

By 1860, before his thirtieth birthday, Ouray had become chief of the entire Yuhtas tribe. He had earned the respect of his tribe, due to his character and ability to lead, and this power proved useful in dealing with the White Man. Ouray looked with dismay upon the invasion of gold prospectors heading over the Continental Divide into Yuhtas territory, and he knew that the White Man would soon take over the ancestral land of his people.

"We do not want to sell a foot of our land; that is the opinion of our people. The Whites can go and take the land and come out again. We do not want them to build houses here." Ouray was a keen observer of human nature. He grasped the challenge of the extreme differences between the Indian and White Man. He learned the politics of the White Man and knew and valued the traditions of his people. Ouray knew that no matter how many battles the Utes might win, they could never stem the tide of the invading Whites. As chief, Ouray chose what he believed was the only path to follow, the diplomatic approach.

He struck a deal with his friend, Kit Carson, a government Indian agent, on March 2nd, 1868. The Kit Carson Treaty, on the surface, seemed a fair deal. It retained for the Yuhtas some six million acres of land. Ouray and his people were guaranteed that "no one would pass over the remaining Yuhtas land." But an exception was added to the agreement that allowed for roads and railways on the Yuhtas land, thus, in fact making the treaty useless to the Utes.

But even this was too little for the needs and greed of the Whites. In *Harpers Weekly*, the headline of October 30th, 1879 read: "The Utes Must Go." Gold had been discovered in Yuhtas territory and the government pushed the Indians aside, once again.

Ouray was put in the untenable position of explaining to his people why they must leave their land. By 1880, the Yuhtas Mountain Indians were moved to reservations by the United States government.

The Yuhtas Mountain Indian reservation stretched from the Four Corners area, east to Pagosa Springs; approximately one hundred ten miles. From the New Mexico border north, the distance was roughly twenty miles, a tiny fraction of their original land. The Utes for their part had dealt in good faith. Now they were confined to a reservation.

Ouray continued to try to serve his people. He and his wife, Chipeta, journeyed to the Southern Yuhtas agency at Ignacio In the summer of 1880. Their goal was to negotiate once again with the White Man. Unfortunately, while Ouray completed the journey, he died without seeing his mission fulfilled. Chief Ouray died on August 24th, 1880. The *Denver Tribune* obituary read:

> In the death of Ouray, one of the historical characters passes away. He has figured quite prominently. Ouray is in many respects . . . a remarkable Indian . . . pure instincts and keen

perception. A friend to the White Man and protector to the Indians.

Today, a southern Colorado town, a mountain, parks, and memorial gardens immortalize Ouray, Chief of the Yuhtas Mountain Indians. He is remembered as one of the great Peace Chiefs in a very sad history of Native American and Euro-American relations.

A House of Prayer for All People

YA'IR FELT STRANGE as he came to the outskirts of this city, which was much larger than anything he had seen in a long while. The city called Denver was full of life and had many streets and multi-story buildings. The rabbi was uncomfortable at the looks that he got as he rode his horse down its well-kept dirt streets. Once he had gotten such looks because of his Hasidic clothing, but now it was because of the clothing he had acquired in the wilderness. To be sure, he still wore *tzitzit* and a *kippah*, but now he carried his *tefillin* in a beaded Cheyenne pipe bag and his *tallit* was folded neatly in a *parfleche* tied to the saddle of his horse.* His dress had become a mix of mountain man, Indian and ranch hand—the people with whom he had lived on the plains and in the mountains of this territory, and with whom he had spent, it seemed, a lifetime. He had become comfortable in the clothes; but now that he was riding through a town with store-fronts, hotels, restaurants, saloons and gambling establishments, he felt odd and out of place again.

Soon he came to a part of town that was not as neat and orderly as the rest. The people looked different from the men he had seen in cravats and coats, the women in

---

* Again, parfleche is a Native American bag (usually of hard leather and colorfully designed) often used for carrying dried meat.

fancy dresses with parasols. Here were men in sombreros and vests, women in skirts and blouses, their hair tied back comfortably. In this part of town, there was noise and laughter. He also noticed that there was a mix of people here—some Indian, some Mexican, some Black, some White, and a smattering of Chinese. Here he felt more comfortable, though he still got a look or two as he rode down the dirt road through this part of town.

He had been drawn to the city of Denver, but for what reason he did not know. Nevertheless, he thought it would be nice to sleep in a bed, to eat good food, and to prepare in comfort for the holiday of Shavuot.

Once again, he was going to celebrate this sacred time by himself. Here he would read from *Humash* and *Siddur* and chant the ancient melodies on his own.[*] He would pray alone, call out to God for wisdom alone, and thank God for making him what he was—a person who, through the process of Pesah and Shavuot, had found true freedom.

While caught-up in the reverie of preparations for the holiday, he suddenly became aware of a man staring at him. The man was wearing a long frock coat and he was Black. It was not a combination he was used to seeing. But stranger than the way the man looked, was the way the man looked at *him*. He was staring hard, and this made the rabbi uncomfortable. Then the man began to grin and suddenly ran toward him yelling: "It's you! It's really you!"

---

[*] A *Humash* is the Torah in a book form, and a *Siddur* is a Jewish prayer book.

Ya'ir almost fell off his horse, not knowing whether to defend himself or flee. But something about the man told him that he was not in danger, but rather in for a hug. And he was right. The Black man reached his horse and jumped up and hugged the rabbi in a way that almost unhorsed him again! When the hug finally subsided, the man exclaimed, "Don't you remember me?"

Ya'ir was embarrassed that he didn't. It was not until the man reached into his shirt and pulled some spices and the remnants of a *Havdalah* candle out of a bag did recognition dawn on the rabbi's face. His mouth fell open, and for a third time, he was almost unhorsed—this time by his own surprise.

"It's you!" he exclaimed with a dumbfounded look. He slid off his horse and, in the middle of the street, the two men embraced. "I'm sorry, I don't remember your name," the rabbi said.

"I'm called Barney Lancelot Ford.* That is the name I chose for myself once I freed myself from slavery. But come with me; let me take you to my house. We can eat, talk some, and catch up; and you can tell my why you're dressed like an Indian, even carrying one of their medicine pouches! Then you can get some rest—you look like you could use it."

---

* Barney Lancelot Ford was an ex-slave and prominent entrepreneur who had a lot to do with the statehood of Colorado. He is immortalized in stained glass in the capital building in Denver.

At this, Reb Yair looked down at the pouch he always carried around his neck and smiled: "Yes, my people call it a *kameyah,* and the leather strap that ties it closed is the gift you gave me so long ago, the remnant of the whip, the symbol of your painful past. I carry it as a reminder and a challenge."

Ya'ir was filled with questions as they walked, leading his horse down the street to a rather large house.

"This is yours?!" he exclaimed in wonder.

Barney laughed, "Yes, I have done well out here."

"In the gold mines?" The rabbi asked.

Barney didn't answer. He took Ya'ir to feed and stable his horse, and then helped the rabbi prepare his food in a kosher manner. Soon, they found themselves sitting at the kitchen table in Barney Ford's house, drinking coffee and eating the chicken that Ya'ir had prepared.

The Black man now explained how he had tried to file two claims, but since he was Black, he wasn't allowed to file on the claims. He hired a couple of lawyers to file for him, but they only ended up stealing the claims from him. Then he made his way to Denver and opened a saloon for the thirsty miners. His liquor was good and he never cheated the miners, so they kept coming back.

"In time, I prospered and bought some land and opened different businesses. Anyway, it's a long story. How long can you stay?"

"To be honest," said the rabbi, "I was planning to stay for a while. You see, soon is a special holiday of my people called Shavuot."

"Is that like *Shabbat?*" Barney interrupted.

"You remembered!" the rabbi laughed.

Barney became very serious and said very quietly, "It changed my life."

There was a poignant moment of silence. Then the rabbi said: "Mr. Ford, you changed mine as well. I would be honored to share Shavuot with you."

"*Uh* . . . Would you mind sharing it with some other folk as well?" asked Barney.

The rabbi was unsure of what his friend meant, but he replied, "With anyone who is willing!"

"Done," Barney said. "Now finish your meal, get some sleep, and we'll talk in the morning."

The next morning, the rabbi went outside to wash and do his morning *davenen*. When he had finished washing, he turned to find that there was a small crowd staring at him! There were Blacks and Whites, Indians and Mexicans, two elderly Chinese gentlemen, women and men, all staring at him. He couldn't remember the last time he had blushed.

Then Barney, who was also there, spoke up and said; "I told them that you were here and they all wanted to see the way you pray."

Then Ya'ir understood. A little self-consciously, the rabbi put on his *tallit* and *tefillin*. He heard people whispering and commenting, but he tried to concentrate and focus on opening himself up to the intention of his actions. Then he began to chant *Shaharit*, the morning prayers. As he got into the readings, the psalms and other parts of the Bible as well, his voice grew in song. To his utter amazement, the people standing behind him began to sing and chant as well. He heard Negro spirituals, Catholic prayers chanted in Spanish, and a mixture of different Indian chants behind him. Somehow, the cacophony didn't seem out of place. He sang louder, and so did they, until the whole area was filled with the spiritual outreaching of many different souls, each with his or her own tradition, blending into something very holy. He felt a shudder of deep fervor move up his spine. For over forty minutes he davened and heard and felt the chants, songs and dancing behind him. When he finally turned from his prayers, he watched mesmerized as the chanting of the eclectic congregation also began to fade away.

His friend Barney was smiling. "They've got the spirit, don't they rabbi!"

"That was the most amazing *davenen* of which I have ever been a part. What is this is about?"

"Well, fair is fair. If you are going to share your Shavuot with us, I'll share with you what this is," Barney said, making a sweeping gesture with his hand to include the people and his house. "When I first escaped from slavery, I thought that I was free. I loved it. I danced and sang and drank and laughed. But soon I felt an emptiness. I realized that I wasn't really free. I thought that if I could make a living, then I could make a life as a free man. So I decided to come West and make my fortune, and I did. But even that was not satisfying enough. Then I began to see that my freedom had no purpose if I didn't have a purpose. So I started classes for anyone who wanted to learn to read and write. At first, my own people filled the classes, but then others came and joined. I opened what I call, 'The Peoples' Restaurant' with open seating for anyone and everyone. People started coming and sharing their needs and helping each other. We meet on Sunday for church services, and anyone can pray any way they like. What you thought was my house is really a house of prayer for all people!" Barney laughed.

Someone chimed in: "And Barney taught us about your *Shabbat* thing. Many of us meet on Friday night for a meal, and on Saturday night too. We study the Bible and the stories of our Red brothers, and some from our brothers from China as well!"

Barney laughed his warm and deep laugh again. "Just as the restaurant is open to everyone, so are our prayer services and classes. It seems to me that freedom is nothing unless you do something with it. Now I live by a code—the code of openness. You had a lot to do with that; I still remember sitting in that cave with you. I was pretty frightened, and you welcomed me. You shared with me. You didn't try to sell me anything or sell me *to* anyone. I saw that, for you, freedom meant serving something higher. You stood up for *me*, so I stand up for *them*," he smiled bashfully. "Look at me, I'm giving a sermon!" But when he looked up at the rabbi, Reb Ya'ir was in tears. "What's wrong?" whispered Barney.

"You've just explained Shavuot better than I could ever have," he said.

Barney grinned. "You're not getting off that easily. You said that tomorrow is Shavuot. We want to learn all about it. What can we do to help?"

"We begin tonight," Ya'ir murmured slowly, his determination growing like the mythical greenery that surrounded Mount Sinai for the time that the Jews waited there for Moshe. "It is called *Tikkun Leil Shavuot*, and it has to do with preparing to receive true freedom. We will need dairy foods—no meats."

Some of the men grumbled a little. But at a glance from Barney, the man who had elevated their lives, they were silent.

"Tonight will be a night of study, I'll bring things from my tradition, from the Torah, the first five books of the Bible, as well as teachings from Psalms and Prophets. Then I'll include some teachings from the Talmud, which is a repository of the teachings of the early Rabbis. And . . . *I have a few more things*" he smiled quizzically. Then he added, "And I hope you will bring any teachings that are truly important to *you*."

One of the men called out, "How 'bout some whiskey?!" The men laughed.

"Well," smiled Reb Ya'ir, "I don't think that's going to help us prepare, and certainly won't increase our awareness, so I think, not this time."

With a look from Barney, the subject was closed. The rest of the day was filled with preparations: butter was churned, cheeses were bought, and fruits and vegetables were brought in from farms on the outskirts of the town.

Word soon began to spread about "strange activities" going on in the 'non-White' part of town. Some women from the other side of town came by to contribute, though their men were none too pleased by it. Nevertheless, some curious men came too, as well as a preacher or two to find out what this Jew was doing with "those people." They were all welcomed by the little community, and everyone helped with the sweeping and cleaning for the evening's convocation.

That night, people began to gather and the lamps were lit. Food was placed out along with coffee and water. They saw the rabbi muttering in a strange language and weaving back and forth.

Barney explained to the newcomers, "He is praying in the old-time language, Hebrew!"

Soon, Reb Ya'ir came to sit with the growing crowd. He was a bit intimidated by all the people. The people he had met in the morning were there, of course, but the numbers had swelled with farmers who had donated the cheese and vegetables, and with some curious townsfolk, women and men who wanted to see what was going on, but were somewhat cautious about their surroundings. A couple of the preachers from the local churches were also there. They stood apart with arms crossed in a little group of men from the 'White' side of town.

The rabbi began by introducing the purpose of the evening's activities. He exclaimed loudly: "My people tell a story about freedom. Some of it comes from the Torah— the first five books of the Bible—and some comes from the teachings of great Rabbis. It goes like this:

"When my people came into the wilderness, after leaving Egypt, they were frightened. What they were leaving had been monstrous, but where they were going was a mystery. They felt that they had no direction; they were following their leader, Moshe, blindly. After 40 days, they came to a small mountain. It was called Mount Sinai. There, they were told to wait, that Moshe was going to the top of the mountain to receive direction for the people. He was going to climb the mountain and come down with Torah, a guide for the people. Moshe said that, in addition, they would hear the directions from God, and that they should prepare.

"Some felt they needed a drink to prepare, and some felt that they needed a good night's sleep before they were to come before God. Others felt that maybe God would come to them in their sleep. For whatever reason, the people overslept. Can you imagine missing an appointment with God? Well, that is what they did. Since that time, according to our tradition, every year before the day of celebrating the receiving of Torah, my people stay awake all night studying, learning, remembering, and preparing to 'receive.'

"You see, Torah is more than a title for the first five books of the Bible. Torah means 'a guide,' direction for our lives. Receiving Torah is, I have learned from my Red brothers, a quest for inner Vision. That is what I intend to do tonight. So I thank you for coming, and I invite you to join me, to share with me and let me share with you. This is a night of Torah sharing. I will share my Torah, and you share your Torah. Let us open our hearts and our souls to a night of preparing to receive a good vision for our lives."

At this, many of the Indians began to nod in agreement. The rabbi asked them to speak and share what they understood. They were a little embarrassed to be called out like this for something that seemed to them to be so natural, but an elder spoke up.

He stood wrapped in his blanket and said: "For my people," he had liked how the Ya'ir had introduced what he said that way, "this is one of the Old Ways. Our people who follow the Old Ways seek visions. They go out into the wilderness and prepare to receive directions for their lives, as the 'Light-giver' says!"

At this, Reb Ya'ir turned quickly to the old man, "How do you know that name?"

The old man smiled, "Because I was there when you visited my tribe. I heard our chief, Ouray call you this name. And that is why I am here. You are a man who listens to the wisdom of others. To me, that says that you have wisdom to share. For a man who listens to others is wise, and his words are worth hearing.

Unnoticed, in the back of the room, one of the preachers was stunned by the simple words of the 'Injun,' as he had often called the native people of this land. He wondered to himself— *How could a teaching of such significance come from a heathen?*

"My people also have words worth hearing. Our land has been taken from us. Treaties have been made and broken," continued the old man, standing wrapped in a striped blanket, one feather hanging from his hair. "Yet I have a vision that, in this land, my people and the teachings of my people will not disappear."

The rabbi smiled: "It is good to see you again, my friend. And your Torah has great power. Your people have been my teachers for many years, and I am grateful for the learning that I have received. I bless you and pray that the *ru'ah*, the wind-spirit of your people will reach out to all the people who call this land their home. Tonight is a night of sharing, for in sharing, each of us shall find his"— then he became acutely aware of the women present— "and *her* own sacred direction."

"And tonight is a night for all to *listen*," said Barney Ford, staring at the hostile faces of some of the men in the back with the two preachers.

A dark skinned man, carrying a sombrero in his hands took a deep breath and said in a deep Hispanic accent: "I would like to share some of my . . . What did you call it? . . .

Torah." Barney smiled at the man who had come to him to learn enough English to get a job, and now taught English to others from Mexico in his school. "I am proud of my history, of my people. I am also proud to be here in *this* country. I have the exalted position of deputy sheriff for the *Mexican* part of town," he announced with appropriate sarcasm. "But my people work hard, and yet, are not treated with respect by the White people of this country. I seek a vision for this land that *my heritage, my people*, and the *way of my people* will be respected."

Then, at the urging of Reb Ya'ir, Barney Ford retold his own story. He spoke of the horror of slavery, of how he had run away and, in hiding, found a White Man who did not want to enslave him, but rather, was willing to share his special day, *Shabbat,* with a runaway slave. He spoke of his search for freedom, the freedom that comes from having a purpose, a direction, not just for himself, but for others. He spoke of his own vision, of which his school and restaurant were small manifestations.

A dark haired woman asked: "Is tonight a night for women too?"

"Of course," answered the rabbi, "we each learn and hear differently. It is important to learn how others hear the sacred teachings. There is a story told by my people that, at Mount Sinai, each person heard God in their own way—men, women and children."

"Good," she said, "for I seek a vision too. I seek a vision where women will be considered equal to men." At this, there was some laughter from the back, as the preacher and his friends scoffed. But she continued: "Women work and think and feel. I have heard of women who teach in universities. And there are women doctors who heal the sick. There are women who lead charities to help the poor. Women raise families. Yet our voices are not heard. We are not even allowed to vote. My vision is of a world where the voice of women will be heard and valued too."

Reb Ya'ir was moved by this, and thought of the Maid of Ludmir, the woman-Rebbe, of whom he had just heard whispers before he left for America.* His mind drifted to that gifted teacher, Hannah Rochel Werbermacher, who had to teach from behind a wall, a *mehitzah* as the separation was called.** Men came from miles around to learn from her, but insisted that she teach them from behind the veil of the *mehitzah*. He wondered how this envisioned equality would affect the people of his 'tribe.' Would the *mehitzah*, which came into existence during Temple times to curtail the secular merriment at sacred gatherings, fall by the wayside; or would his people, as they were so often wont to do, find creative solutions from tradition to the challenges of an ever-changing world. He looked up suddenly, realizing that his mind had taken him

---

* See "Precocious Mystical Feminism" in Zalman Schachter-Shalomi, *Wrapped in a Holy Flame: Teachings and Tales of the Hasidic Masters,* San Francisco: Jossey-Bass, 2003.

** A *mehitzah* is a partition between men and women in an Orthodox synagogue or *shul*. In the Orthodox view of spirituality, it is not meant as an insult, but rather as a recognition of separate roles played by men and women.

from this place to the shtibls of his youth. People were staring at him and waiting for his response.

"I'm sorry," the rabbi said, "my mind drifted as I thought of the challenge that our sister has put before us. I hear your Torah," he said. "I believe that with your fervor and dedication, the government will grant your vision, for I have found that wisdom and truth are found in both sexes, in all people. In the Bible we find the great wisdom of Ruth, Hannah, Tamar, Miriam and Devorah, to name just a few of the women who were teachers and leaders of my tribe. May the hearts of men be open to the teachings of women!"

Throughout the night, many people shared their Torah. Periodically, the rabbi would add some words or tell a story. As the morning dawned, and most of the people had shared, the rabbi stood up and began to speak: "When my people left Egypt, they began a process of *becoming* free. But it was at Sinai, on this day, that the true meaning of freedom came to light. Freedom doesn't merely mean the end of slavery; it means finding purpose in liberty."

But before the rabbi could continue, a preacher who had stayed the whole night standing in the diminishing number of Whites who had come to deride the proceedings, interrupted.

People looked at him with distrust and hostility, for he said: "I did not come here to share: I came here because I thought this was a dangerous meeting of heretics and nonbelievers. I was ready to have the sheriff come and break up the meeting."

At this there were definite rumblings from the people. But the preacher continued: *"But I was wrong.* I have heard wisdom and true faith from Christian, non-Christian, and even from those I would have called heathen. What did you call it, Rebbe? (He pronounced it like Bee-Bee). *Torah?* I understand what you mean by freedom. For Christians, it means serving; for we all need to serve. When we serve a higher purpose—I call it serving Jesus—we are truly free. If Jesus were here today, he would be sitting among you. And I would like to sit among you too, if you would allow it."

Barney Ford went over to the preacher and put out his hand. There was a slight hesitation, but the preacher took his hand. Smiles lit the room up like the morning sun. The preacher continued: "I may lose my flock for saying this, but everyone here is welcome in my church, and I hope you will allow me to be part of what you are doing as well."

Reb Ya'ir smiled and said, "The visions that have been shared this night have helped us all to see something very powerful. True freedom comes when we climb the holy mountain of purpose and dedicate ourselves to our visions. That is the meaning of Shavuot. This night we have shared the visions of Torah in the different ways. The Torah that was shared could be cooked up as one simple sentence. I am sure our new friend, the preacher knows exactly where it can be found in the Bible. *V'a'havta L'Rey'akha Kamokha*—'Love your neighbor as yourself.'

The preacher piped in, "Matthew 5:43."

And Reb Ya'ir added, "For my tribe, Leviticus 19:18."

Others shared versions of that simple and powerful phrase. Men and women of different tribes shared that it was a teaching they had learned in childhood. Others remembered hearing it at church. The rabbi smiled: "Just as the story goes—everyone heard God speaking from the mountain in their own ways, so tonight have we shared the Torah that we have heard in our own ways. May we always be open to hearing the Torah of all people, while preserving our own ways." There was a chorus of "Amen!"

Barney Ford embraced the rabbi and the preacher. "It seems to me that we have begun our journey to the holy mountain of freedom," he said, his voice quivering with emotion. "We have sought the visions, now I pray that we will live them."

As the rabbi began his morning *davenen* again, most of the people left to get some rest or to discuss the extraordinary events of the night. But some stayed for a while to watch and, in their own way, participate in what the rabbi was doing. Reb Ya'ir remembered a teaching from his Rebbe back in P'shyskha, Reb Zalman: "Shavuot comes to reminds us that the redemption from slavery was not complete until we received the Torah." On that night, that *Tikkun Leil Shavuot* in Denver, Reb Ya'ir had once again stood at Sinai and received Torah. The Torah that he had received had been from many different 'parchments.' His own Torah parchment stood in the center, with the torah of others all around—some in

Spanish, some in the tribal tongues, some from that faraway place called China, and some from as close as the women standing among them. And, once again, he thanked and praised God, the source of holiness and wholeness, for the many teachers he had encountered along his Torah journey, his Vision Quest, through this promising land.

To Remember the Stories

HER NAME WAS MARY, though she hated the White name the school had assigned her. She remembered her tribal name, *Strong Wind*, the name her parents had given her before the Whites had taken her from her family to be raised in the 'Christian School.' Now her days were filled with learning the White language and the White ways and the White religion. She lived in a crowded dormitory with children taken from many different tribes: Lakota, Blackfoot, Ute, Comanche, Cherokee and others. The only thing that they had in common was what they were learning in this missionary school, that they were all stolen from their families, their homes, their tribes, and that they all hated where they were. And yet, in this foreign place, with a foreign language and foreign customs, there was one bright spot. Every Friday night, the boys and girls would sneak into the girl's dormitory and share. They shared stories and tales from their tribes. They listened and shared, and vowed to remember the stories of their people and their tribal ways.

These sharings were dangerous, because they were breaking the rules of the school. They were not allowed to talk of their past, and they certainly were not allowed out after curfew to tell the old stories and share the sacred memories of their people. If they were caught by the headmistress, it would mean whippings all around with a switch. The headmistress, wife of the headmaster, was very harsh and cruel when she thought that they were sliding backward into their "pagan ways." When the whippings came, it was a point of pride that no child would cry out or beg. Worse then the beatings was the punishment of the headmaster. He would bring them into his smelly office and, with tears in his eyes over their failures, would lecture them from his sacred word book and tell them how the Whites were only trying to civilize them to live in the White world. The lectures would go on and on. It was the general consensus among the children that they would rather have the whippings then these long, solemn lectures.

Even with the threats of beatings and boring lectures, the children would dare to sneak out every Friday night. And every Friday night they would sit and tell stories from their own tribes, stories of bravery in battle, stories of mystical shamans and exciting buffalo hunts. They would tell love stories of how their parents had met each other, and their own tribal creation stories, and stories of how they became who they were. These were sacred stories, and some were very similar even from different tribes. The stories evoked muted laughter and tears, joy and memory and sorrow. Sometimes they would retell stories, taking turns telling stories from each other's tribes. It wasn't important whose story it was; it was only important 'to remember.'

One Friday night, the children were laughing after a funny story of how the beaver outsmarted a White hunter. All of a sudden, the door burst open and there stood the headmistress with a switch in her hand. She yelled at the children, calling them "heathens" and "uncivilized, ungrateful whelps." The children sat calmly, stoically. Then she called out: "Mary! You're behind all of this heathen claptrap; come with me immediately!"

Mary stood up, and with quiet dignity, and an eye on the switch, followed the headmistress out of her room and down the hall to the stairwell. They marched down three flights of stairs to the office of the headmaster. Strong Wind groaned to herself, she would rather have been beaten by this cruel woman than have to sit and listen to the whining voice of the headmaster. She knew what to expect; it wasn't the first lecture that she had received. And sure enough, he began to drone on and on as tears fell from his face as he lectured her on the right way, the Christian way to live.

Finally, after what seemed like days, he exhausted himself. He looked through moist eyes at her and asked: "Why are you so willful and disobedient? Why were you all out after curfew telling those heathen stories?"

Usually, she would have remained silent. It was a teaching that she had learned early in life, to be silent and to wait. And besides, if she answered it would only prolong the torture. But this time she was too angry to let his attack on her people go unanswered. She responded: "We were sharing stories of our people, our Spirit-path, our ways of life. You are trying to steal those memories from us and we will fight you by remembering. Our stories keep us in the Sacred Hoop of Life. And we will continue to share every Friday night, and you will not stop us Reverend Haman!" (She pronounced this, Hay-man.)

The Reverend had heard the kids refer to him as Haman and wondered if it was a coincidence. "Why do you call me Haman?" he asked.

Strong Wind answered: "It is a story that I heard from the Black Hat, the White Man who would visit with my father. He would come, and some of the people would share stories of our people and he would share stories of his. He loved hearing our stories and he learned them. He treated us with respect, and so we treated him in the same way. He shared stories with us. They were wonderful stories about a place far away called "Iz-reel." He told us of a fiery mountain, and a scroll of teachings. He told us stories of a man with a staff who saved his people. And he told us of a man named Mordechai and his cousin Esther and the evil man who wanted to destroy them, Haman. Haman wanted to destroy Mordechai's people, as you are trying to do to us. But Mordechai and Esther tricked him, and he was destroyed. But if Esther had not remembered the stories of her people, they would have been lost. I learned from the Black Hat's story that the only way we can stop you from erasing us from the land is to remember and share our stories!"

Of course, the headmaster was saddened to hear himself compared to the vicious Haman in the Biblical book of Esther. And yet he was intrigued. He asked her to tell him more about Mordecai and Esther and Haman.

She looked at him suspiciously, wondering what trick he was playing. But then she closed her eyes and simply let the story flood back into her mind. She pictured the Black Hat—What was his name again? She didn't remember. Her father had called him, "Light Giver," as he told the story in her father's *tipi* on one cold winter night:

"The people of Iz-reel were stolen from their homes and taken to a faraway place, as you have taken us from our lodges. But though they were far from home, they remembered their stories and their sacred ways. They would meet and tell stories and keep their traditions; and that is what kept them alive. Mordechai was the peace chief of the tribe and his cousin lived in his tipi. Her name was Esther, and she loved listening to the stories of her people.

"There came a time when the Chief of the Persians, the ones who had taken her and so many others from their land, wanted to take a bride. Many women came to the chief's *tipi*, but they were turned away. Mordechai told Esther to go to the chief's *tipi* and to stand outside and wait. She put on her best clothes and went and waited. The chief came out and saw her and fell in love. Soon they were married. Esther cared for the chief, but she cared for her people more. Often, she would sneak out and go to listen to her uncle tell the stories of her people. Though she was married to the chief of the Persians, she never forgot that she was of the tribe of Iz-reel, and she remembered the stories of her people.

"It happened that there was a war chief of the Persians named Haman, who hated Mordechai and his people, the people of Iz-reel. He connived to trick the Chief of the Persians into letting him kill all of the Iz-reel people. When Mordechai heard of his plans, he told Esther that she was the only one who could save the people. She was afraid, but she was very brave. So she made a feast for her husband the chief, and even invited the evil war chief Haman. Her husband ate the wonderful feast, and when he had finished and was in a happy mood, he offered his bride many presents . . . but she would not accept. When the chief asked what she would accept as a gift, she responded: 'My husband, I only want one thing. If you will grant me but one wish, I would be happy!'

" 'What may I offer you?' asked the chief.

" 'I ask only for my life and the life of my people!'

" 'Who would dare to threaten you, my beloved wife?' asked the astonished chief.

"Esther pointed to the evil war chief. 'That man wants to kill me and all of my people who live with your tribe.'

"The chief was so angry that he had the evil war chief killed. And he told all the people in the land of the evil of the war chief. There was a great battle and the tribe of Iz-reel, with the help of the Persians, killed all the evil ones of the war chief Haman in a great battle that took place within the tribe.

"I remember the story just as I have told it to you," said Strong Wind. She looked up defiantly at the headmaster and was astonished to see a smile growing on his tearful face. He called in his wife, who was just as amazed at the look on her husband's face. But she was more amazed at what he said next.

"From now on, every Friday night, the children are to be allowed to tell their stories and to use their birth names, their tribal names. In addition, from now on, this girl will not be known to us as 'Mary.' No, she will be known as 'Esther,' 'Esther the teacher.' For this night she has taught me a lesson. I will no longer be Haman, but rather I shall strive to be Ahasuerus"

Strong Wind was astounded. She could never say that funny name of the Chief of the Persians. *How did the headmaster know it?* she wondered. But she had little time to ponder the question. The headmaster turned to Strong Wind, who was now also Esther. "I must ask you, Esther, why did you choose Friday night to tell your stories?" he inquired.

Strong Wind, who was almost made speechless by the turn of events, waited a moment until she could pull herself together: "The Black Hat, the 'Light Giver' told us that his special day was called '*Shabbat.*' He said it began when the sun had gone to sleep on the day you call 'Friday.' He told us that *Shabbat* lasted all night, and all of the day you call 'Saturday.' Then, when the stars come out to dance in the night of Saturday, the *Shabbat* ended. To him, it was a special time. So I decided to honor him as he had honored my people. Our stories would be told on his *Shabbat.* I shared with the others, whom you have taken far from their homes and tribes, the stories of this man, this Black Hat who lives in peace with all people. I wanted them to know that not all White Men are enemies. I told them so that they would join in the teaching and sharing that is the remembering of our peoples. Maybe you can learn as well, that the path of the peace chief, though a difficult path, is a path that we must all learn to walk."

"How can we learn to walk that path together?" asked the headmaster.

She thought for a minute, and then Strong Wind answered: "The only way that anyone can walk that path is if we all walk it together. The only way that we may stand on the path of the Peace Chiefs is if we are proud of who we are and find joy in the differences between all the peoples. We must respect each other if we are to respect the Great Spirit who created us all."

The headmaster and headmistress were silent. They excused Strong Wind and allowed her to return to her dormitory room. The headmaster and his wife sat and thought of the lessons this young girl had shared. Both her names suited her, thought the headmaster. She is truly Esther who will save her people from extinction. And she will succeed because she has the tenacity, the power of her name, Strong Wind.

From that day forward, every Friday night, the children would tell their tales and laugh and cry together, remembering. And at every gathering, sitting quietly in the back, was the headmaster, learning the tribal ways of these powerful children.

A Guide to the Jewish Holidays

Yamim Noraim (pp. 77-85, 103-115)

THE *YAMIM NORAIM* are awesome days, so much so that Jews refer to them as the "Days of Awe." The term has several understandings. Most literally, it refers to the days encompassing Rosh HaShanah, Yom Kippur and the ten days in between. These days are so powerful to the Jewish people that they are sometimes referred to as *Aseret Yemei Tshuvah'*, which is traditionally translated as 'The Ten Days of Repentance.' Since the word *t'shuvah* comes from the word *shuv,* meaning 'to return,' my translation is 'The Ten Days of Return.' In common parlance, this time period is called 'The High Holy Days.' This period of time is set aside for intense inner reflection, a regaining of spiritual balance, and clearing out of last year's baggage as we prepare for the coming year.

Rosh HaShanah (pp.103-115)

Rosh Hashanah literally means 'head of the year,' and is commonly referred to as 'The Jewish New Year.' It is the beginning of the High Holy Days, or the *Yamim Noraim.* Therefore, it is the beginning of ten intense days of introspection and rebalancing the soul. Rosh Hashanah is observed by most Jews on the first two days of Tishrei, which is the seventh month of the Hebrew calendar. Therefore, it is not literally the 'New Year.'

Rosh Hashanah is found in the Torah: "In the seventh month, on the first day of the month, you shall observe complete rest, a sacred occasion commemorated with loud blasts. You shall not work at your occupations; and you shall bring an offering by fire to *Adonai*" (Leviticus 23:24-25). Our understanding of that passage is that on Rosh Hashanah we do no work, we hear the *shofar* (ram's horn), and take part in a service of worship. In Numbers it states again: "In the seventh month, on the first day of the month, you shall observe a sacred occasion: you shall not work at your occupations . . . You shall observe it as a day when the horn is sounded. You shall present a burnt offering of pleasing odor to *Adonai,*" (Numbers 29:1-2) reiterating the sacred importance of the day. These are traditional translations that reflect the importance to our people of the number 7 (seventh month), the new moon and the desire to mark a 'half-way' point in the year for introspection and prayer. It is the original 'time-out.' It is a time to step back from our daily work, to hear the sharp blasts of *shofar* which might be a call to wake up from our daily routine and to reach out to the sacred.

Yom Kippur (pp.77-85)

Yom Kippur is traditionally translated as 'The Day of Atonement.' It is the second holiest day (after *Shabbat*) of the year for the Jewish people. Its central themes are atonement and repentance. It is mentioned in Torah in Leviticus 23: 27: "On the tenth day of this seventh month is the day of atonement; there shall be a holy convocation for you, and you shall afflict (the word *enetem* can also mean 'to answer,' 'to turn' or 'to humble,' giving the sentence from Leviticus more options for understanding) your souls; and you shall bring an offering made by fire to *Adonai*." We traditionally observe this holy day with a 25-hour period of fasting and intensive prayer, often spending most of the day in synagogue services. Yom Kippur completes the annual period of the High Holy Days, the Days of Awe.

    Yom Kippur is the tenth day of the month of Tishrei. According to Jewish tradition, God inscribes each person's fate for the coming year into "The Book of Life" on Rosh Hashanah, and waits until Yom Kippur to "seal" the verdict. During the Days of Awe, Jews seek to release the baggage of guilt and anger and to redirect our path. We seek forgiveness for moving off the path of our relationship with God. This is called *Bain HaAdam L'Makom*, the private soul work done between God and the person. Where we have hurt and been hurt by other human beings is referred to as *Bain Adam LeHavero*, between one person and another. And we seek to forgive others and be forgiven for our *mis-deeds*, deeds that 'missed the mark' of good relationships. Both are part of the sacred process of the *Yamim Noraim*, which end with Yom Kippur.

    In playing with the word 'atonement,' we create a time to seek *at-one-ment* and *attunement*. The evening and day of Yom Kippur are set-aside for public and private prayer, petitions, meditations and confessions *(viddui)*. At the end of Yom Kippur, if we have been successful, we feel a level of joy and comfort. Some consider themselves absolved by God. Others would say that we have brought God deeper into our lives for the coming year.

Sukkot (pp.27-39)

Sukkot is referred to, in secular and Christian writings as "The Feast of Booths" or "The Feast of Tabernacles." It is of Biblical origin, and is celebrated on the 15th day of the Fall month of Tishrei. It is one of the three biblically mandated pilgrimage festivals called the *Shalosh Regalim*, on which Jews in ancient times would make pilgrimages to the Temple to worship and share feasts and fellowship. It is the last of the harvest festivals before the long cold and, we hope, wet winter. The festival lasts seven days, including the first day. The intermediate days are called *Hol HaMo'ed*, and are immediately followed by another festive day known as *Shemini Atzeret*, 'The Last Great Day.'

It has a third meaning that is emphasized by the name itself. The Hebrew the word Sukkot is the plural of *sukkah*, 'booth' or 'tabernacle,' which is a walled or tent like structure, the roof left open, only covered with flora, such as tree branches or bamboo shoots. Originally, they were covered with date palm leaves, which are plentiful in Israel and can be found even in the desert. The *sukkah* is a memory peg. For some, it symbolizes the fragile dwelling in which our ancient ancestors dwelt during their 40 years of wandering in the desert after the Exodus from Egypt. For others it symbolizes God's comforting cloud cover during that same period.

Throughout the holiday, the *sukkah* becomes the primary living area of one's home. For some, all meals are eaten inside the *sukkah,* and we sleep there as well. For others, the symbolic eating of bread in the *sukkah* fulfills the sacred connection or commandment *(mitzvah)*. On each day of the holiday, we bring a bundle of three species of plant, and a citron to wave after first reciting a blessing over the bundle we call *lulav* and *etrog*. The four components are: the citron, called an *etrog;* thin leafy branches of the willow called *aravot;* myrtle called *hadasim;* and the date palm branch called *lulav.*

Living in this temporary and seemingly fragile shelter reminds Jews of the fragility and the strength of life. It challenges us to look at those who have less, and to seek ways to care for the poor and the stranger.

Hoshanah Rabbah (pp.69-75)

As Sukkot comes to an end, there is a small, powerful holiday, a call for mercy at the end of the season that begins with Rosh HaShanah. Hoshanah Rabbah, which means 'The Great Call for Salvation' is the last moment, the procrastinator's holy day of return to balance, or in traditional terms, to repent. The season which officially began on the 1st of Tishrei, or in most traditions as early as a month before, ends on Hoshanah Rabbah on the 21st day of Tishrei. We have a special service marked with unique rituals, including dancing around the *bimah* or the Ark or the synagogue carrying our *lulav* and *etrog* while chanting special supplications called *Hoshanot*.

It is customary for the scrolls of the Torah to be removed from the ark during this procession and carried in these circuits called *Hakafot*. In a few communities, a *shofar* is sounded after each circuit. Also, in some communities, congregants leave their *lulavim* at the synagogue, never bringing thing them back into their homes. Some people, myself included, keep *lulavim* and *etrogim* all year long as household decorations, and use the *etrogim* for spice boxes used in *Havdalah* (see *Shabbat*) by pushing cloves into the skin of the *etrog*. Others will make *etrog* jelly or *etrog* liquor and believe it to be of spiritual aid for women who wish to conceive.

Simhat Torah

Simhat Torah is all about endings that become beginnings. Simhat Torah falls on the day after Hoshanah Rabbah. In synagogue, the last *parsha* (portion) of the Torah is read and then immediately following, the first *parsha* of the Torah is read creating a complete circle of readings. During this joyful ceremony, people dance with the Torah as we all make seven circuits (*hakafot*). Simhat Torah marks the end of the time of *t'shuvah* (return/repentance). It is also a remembrance of our agricultural roots, as we begin to add a blessing for rain for the land of Israel, which is so dependent upon rain for survival (there being only one river in Israel). The blessing—indeed the entire holiday—is about hope for the future of a people, a land, and a planet.

Hannukhah (pp.41-68)

Hannukhah is often called 'The Festival of Lights,' and though it is a minor festival, it has become one of the most joyous times of the Jewish year. The reason for the celebration has to do with human endeavor and divine intervention. This holiday has a date in history, approximately 165 B.C.E.. Hannukhah celebrates the miraculous military victory of the small, ill-equipped Jewish guerilla army over the ruling Greek Syrians under Antiochus, who had banned the Jewish religion and desecrated the Temple. Hannukhah celebrates the unique war fought solely for religious freedom. Hannukhah celebrates the miracle of a small cruse of sacred oil, used to keep the *Menorah,* our *Ner Tamid* (regularly lit lamp). When the Jews returned from the war to clean the desecrated Temple, they found that there was but one small cruse of oil left. It was not expected to last one day, and yet it lasted eight days, until more oil could be processed. The *mitzvot* of Hannukhah are: 1) to light the *hannukiyah* (nine branch candelabra or *menorah)* for eight nights with olive oil or wax candles (following ancient tradition, on each succeeding night, one more candle is added to the *hannukiyah* and lit); 2) interestingly enough, it is also a *mitzvah* to eat food fried in oil (for some this is potato pancakes, *latkes,* and for others, it is jelly doughnuts, *sufganiyot).* It is also a custom to play with a *dreidel,* a four-sided top with a letter on each side. The letters stand for the phrase: "A great miracle happened there." In Israel, one of the letters is different and the meaning is: "A great miracle happened *here*."

Purim (pp.155-162)

The story of Purim comes to us from *Megillat Esther*, 'The Scroll of Esther.' It is the story of tragedy averted, courage and faith. The players are Esther who becomes queen and saves the Jewish people; King Ahasuerus, the unaware king, who is maneuvered by his wicked advisor, Haman; and Esther's uncle (or cousin) Mordechai, the who calls on Esther to save the people.

This springtime holiday is celebrated with costumes and laughter and noise as we read the *Megillah* and add an extra prayer for salvation. One reason for the added silliness may be that we were saved from genocide, or maybe it is because this is the only book in the *TaNaKh* (Bible) in which God is not mentioned.

Pesah (pp.87-102)

Pesah is actually the first holy day of the Jewish Year. It is celebrated in the spring on the 15th of the first Jewish month, Nisan. There are three powerful and intertwined components. Most notably, Pesah celebrates the Exodus, the leaving of Egypt by a large group of slaves, reaching out for freedom and faith. It also celebrates the first harvest of the new year. After a the long, cold Winter, filled with prayers for rain, the first crops are ready to be harvested. It is a time of great joy and celebration, and a deep recognition of the cycle of the year, nature and the source of all. It is celebrated for seven days in Israel, and eight days everywhere else. Lastly, it is a holiday with a temporal moral lesson. Over and over in Torah, it says that we are to treat the stranger with compassion and caring, and always with the refrain: "for you were slaves in the land of Egypt!"

The story, which begins in the second book of the Torah, paints a picture of the downtrodden Jewish people saved by the hero and prophet Moshe, who follows faithfully the directions of God. It begins with Pharaoh's stubbornness, even in the face of ten plagues inflicted on him and his people. The last plague was that of the death of the firstborn son of all the people in Egypt. God instructs the people through Moshe to put lamb's blood on their *mezuzot* (doorposts). The Messenger of Death passes over (in Hebrew *pasha*, from which Pesah, 'Passover' is derived) the houses of the Jews. Pharaoh relents for the moment and the Jews prepare to flee. The night before their flight, the Jews ate meals of lamb and *matzah* and then, in the morning, fled. We are taught that the people carried the dough for bread on their backs so it didn't have a chance to rise. Therefore, the holiday is called "The Festival of the Unleavened Bread," though that name could also speak to the harvest festival. The unleavened bread is called *matzah* and is the primary symbol of the holiday.

Pesah, like Shavuot (Pentecost) and Sukkot (Tabernacles) are called *Hagim*, meaning pilgrimage festivals. As Muslims have the *Haj*, a pilgrimage to Mecca, in ancient times, Jews were to make the pilgrimage to

Jerusalem three times a year. The three *Hagim* are called the *Shalosh Regalim*.

Shavuot (pp.137-154)

Shavuot is the feast of 'Weeks' because it falls on the week of weeks (49 days) after the beginning of Pesah. Shavuot also has three meanings. It commemorates the anniversary of the day God gave Torah to the Jewish people at Mount Sinai, and thus is called *Z'man Matan Torah*, 'The Time of the Giving of Torah.' It also is the day of the second harvest. And lastly, it is a holiday that speaks to an awareness of our dependence on the Earth and our need for faith. The holiday is one of the *Shalosh Regalim*, the three biblical pilgrimage festivals.

The date of Shavuot is directly linked to that of Passover. The Torah calls us to make a seven-week Counting of the Omer (lit. sheaf), beginning on the second day of Passover and immediately followed by Shavuot. This counting of days and weeks expresses our faith, based anticipation and desire for Torah. It is viewed as our wedding to the service of God. In Torah, it is also called'Tthe Festival of Reaping,' *Had HaKitsur* (Exodus 23:16), and 'Day of the First Fruits,' *Yom HaBikkurim*, (Numbers 28:26).

Shabbat (pp.13-25)

Shabbat is the most important of Jewish Holy Days and comes every week beginning at sundown on Friday night and ends when three stars are visible on Saturday night, after approximately 26 hours. It is a time of rest and study and prayer. Services are held in synagogues on Friday evening and Saturday morning. It is a time when Jews turn from the workaday week to the holy day of being. It celebrates life, the creation of the world, as well as an awareness of the power and importance of freedom. Slaves do not have a Shabbat, and the holy day reminds us that we were once slaves, and that no one should be enslaved to anyone nor anything. Shabbat has power to refresh, replenish, and to put life in perspective. On Shabbat, every week a section of Torah is read at services and studied at home, accompanied by three meals and an avoidance of the mundane.

Shabbat begins with the lighting of candles, the drinking of wine and the eating of *hallah* (egg bread). It ends with the ceremony of *Havdalah*, and the lighting of a multi-wicked candle, the drinking of wine, and the smelling of sweet spices to keep this special day in our memory during the coming week.

The Jewish Calendar

The Jewish calendar has the following months:

Hebrew	Number	Length	Civil Equivalent
Nissan	1	30 days	March-April
Iyar	2	29 days	April-May
Sivan	3	30 days	May-June
Tammuz	4	29 days	June-July
Av	5	30 days	July-August
Elul	6	29 days	August-September
Tishri	7	30 days	September-October
Heshvan	8	29/30 days	October-November
Kislev	9	30/29 days	November-December
Tevet	10	29 days	December-January
Shevat	11	30 days	January-February
Adar	12	30 days	February-March
Adar II (lp. yr.)	13	29 days	February-March

About the Author

RABBI BAHIR DAVIS is from a rabbinic family that includes his grandfather, father and brother. He studied to become a rabbi at various yeshivas in the United States and Israel and holds two *smikhot* (ordination certificates): one signed by rabbis from many branches of Judaism, including the late Rabbi Alexander Schindler *zt'l*, past President of the Union of Reform Judaism; and another from the founder of the Jewish Renewal movement, Rabbi Zalman Schachter-Shalomi. Reb Bahir is a *maggid* (storyteller) in the best tradition of Jewish storytelling and is known for his vibrant humor and imagery. His eclectic background and study of Zen Buddhism, Japanese culture, Aikido, and Native American culture inform his approach to Judaism and have opened up many insights on the nature of the Jewish path. He has worked with numerous outreach programs, held the post of Executive Director of the Introduction to Judaism Program for the Union of Reform Judaism, and has served as a congregational rabbi. Reb Bahir is not connected with any one movement, preferring to serve the entire spectrum of the Jewish community. He is currently the spiritual leader of Rocky Mountain Hai, based in Lafayette, Colorado.

www.ingramcontent.com/pod-product-compliance
Lightning Source LLC
Chambersburg PA
CBHW070148100426
42743CB00013B/2852